AHMED FROM AMERICA

AHMED FROM AMERICA

Edward Muesch

iUniverse, Inc.
New York Bloomington Shanghai

AHMED FROM AMERICA

iUniverse books may be ordered through booksellers or by contacting:

iUniverse
1663 Liberty Drive
Bloomington, IN 47403
www.iuniverse.com
1-800-Authors (1-800-288-4677)

Because of the dynamic nature of the Internet, any Web addresses or links contained in this book may have changed since publication and may no longer be valid.

The views expressed in this work are solely those of the author and do not necessarily reflect the views of the publisher, and the publisher hereby disclaims any responsibility for them.

ISBN: 978-0-595-49930-4 (pbk)
ISBN: 978-0-595-49885-7 (cloth)
ISBN: 978-0-595-61310-6 (ebk)

Printed in the United States of America

This book is dedicated to my first mate and wife, Helen, who has remained nearby to weather every storm. I have crossed many oceans and continents with her always at my side.

I also wish to dedicate this book to the many people I encountered on the street and whose names and identities I sometimes changed to protect them. It was their honesty and willingness to speak freely that made it possible to write this book.

CONTENTS

Acknowledgments

I wish to acknowledge the following people and organizations that played an important part in helping me bring *Ahmed from America* to publication:

Tolga and Oslem Toprak, of Akustik Travel, Bodrum, Turkey, who arranged and coordinated our travels throughout eastern Turkey during a period when few people went there.

The Eastern Mediterranean Rally, whose organizers provided around-the-clock support, and coordination, and made our journey to North Cyprus, Syria, Lebanon, Israel, and Egypt under sail possible. Our special thanks and appreciation to Hasan Kacmaz, Dave and Kath Gerard, Faruk Gunlu and Umut Tepedelenlioglu, without whom I would have never been able to interview the people and visit these exotic countries.

Also by Edward Muesch:

Rising Above the Wave
Personal Best: Chasing the Wind Above and Below the Equator
The Land of Men

Introduction

After many years working as a director of engineering for a major U.S. corporation, I made the decision to retire early and pursue my personal goal to sail around the world. Like many woman sailors, my wife, Helen, became my first mate with some trepidation about leaving family and friends for an extended period of time. Once at sea, she quickly adapted to her new life, and we shared the adventure together. During our circumnavigation, Helen and I almost drowned in the 2004 tsunami at Phi Phi Don Island, Thailand. The emotional toll this one event took on our lives was far beyond anything we were prepared for. Even several years after the tsunami, we continue to struggle with the aftermath of what happened. We're often asked how the tsunami changed our lives. Without going into detail, we can say our lives have never been the same since that fateful day. One positive outcome for me has been the need to write and attempt to share those things that have become most important to me in life.

Nearing the end of our circumnavigation, we reached Turkey aboard our sailboat *Tahlequah*. We felt it was time to stop, rest, and recover before crossing the Atlantic and completing our journey. Because we had come so close to death, we both realized that every hour now counted, and we needed to make the most of our lives. Helen and I felt welcome and at home in Turkey. We jointly decided to stay at a marina aboard our sailing vessel.

We had on many occasions discussed purchasing a home in the United States versus one elsewhere. Helen decided she didn't want to purchase a home in the States; she would rather have one in Turkey. This was in part due to our having five children in the States with whom we could visit for brief periods. Our daughter and son-in-law in North Carolina had made the first floor of their home available to us for visiting and we had rooms in the homes of our other children in Georgia and New Jersey.

In a timely fashion, we received a phone call from our close Turkish friend, Uri, saying he had found a home in Bodrum we should consider buying. Uri took us to see it, and Helen fell in love with the home; it was love at first sight.

Our first view from the rear of the house and garden was breathtaking. Being there at sunset, we saw the many Turkish and Greek islands in the distance as the sun set behind them. At sunset, streams of yellowish-pinkish-tinted colored ribbons radiated from behind the descending fireball into the sea. A passing cloud created a prism-like effect, dividing the light spectrum into many more shades of yellow and pink. At the final moment, there was a bright burst of yellow, changing into a dark red, as the sun disappeared into the horizon, and day became dusk.

We bought the house. At the bottom of the mountain, there is a private beach belonging to the complex. The house is modern, with marble floors, new utilities, an attached private apartment, fireplace, furnishings, and it is in immaculate condition. It appears to be the perfect place to continue my hobby of writing books, while Helen reads hers. The yacht club where we keep *Tahlequah* is visible in the distance from our garden and patio.

I needed a new purpose in life. Writing has always been a release for me, a distraction that allows me to express my innermost feelings and emotions. I don't write to support myself financially but to support my craving for self-expression and the need to be heard above the everyday noise. Having already written and published one book, I began to consider a second book—a book that would allow me to share how traveling throughout the world has changed my perspective of other people and cultures. I wanted this to be a contribution to people's understanding of the world, even if only in some small way. I didn't want to write a travel guide, but instead a validation of how the Western world forms preconceived ideas of third-world countries. I wanted to offer an alternative to mainstream journalism through the collaborative action of recording the thoughts of everyday people I would encounter on the street. Although I was not a journalist and had no experience in these things, I intended to seek the truth by asking a few of the same questions that journalists ask. Although not entirely sure of how to go about this, I determined I would start by seeking out the average person I would meet in my travels. I wondered if I would receive the same answers and arrive at the same conclusions I'd previously come to.

I decided to travel to the countries and places that as an American I had long ago dismissed as enemies of the West. To begin, I decided to visit the eastern areas of Turkey along the Iraqi and Iranian borders to test my theory that most people are peaceful. Not being a journalist, I had to fall back upon my experience of many years visiting foreign countries and working professionally with foreign people.

One question I asked myself was, why would people respond differently to me than they would to a professional journalist? I suspected that by putting a camera and microphone in front of a person, I encouraged them to feel it was necessary to make a major political or social declaration. I wondered if they would respond in the same way when asked similar questions during a routine conversation without a camera and microphone. As an average American, I wanted to know how citizens of other countries felt about Americans.

In today's American political environment, the average person has begun to see value in "village meetings." People have become intent upon asking their own questions without the filter of a journalist to ask these questions for them. Perhaps because the politician is responding directly to those who will decide their future, their responses often sound more sincere, direct, and honest. It is this example that has convinced me each of us has the right to decide who our friends are and who are not in the world today. Eastern Turkey and the Mideast will be my focus.

Walking the streets of a small Turkish town near Diyarbakir, we came upon a small shop, whose aisles were cluttered. The shop had a musty odor and lighting barely sufficient to see the many items on the shelves. In a back room, my wife Helen discovered camel saddles and attempted to bargain with the shopkeeper.

"There's time to discuss price. First, I will make us tea. You like Turkish tea?" the shopkeeper asked.

"Of course, we love Turkish tea," Helen responded.

"Good, then I will get us some," the man said, as he walked to a corner of the room where two pots, one on top of the other, were brewing tea. He proceeded to allow it to steep a few minutes before pouring our tea into small Turkish glasses, as is the custom.

"I was a colonel in the Turkish army," he announced proudly.

He wore baggy black Turkish village pants and a cotton shirt. Knowing he had been a commissioned military officer in the Turkish army, I tried to imagine him in his dress uniform. He was a cheerful fellow, who appeared to want to talk more than sell us merchandise in his shop.

The three of us sat in the back of the shop to talk. Although wanting to know where we were from and how we liked eastern Turkey, he also wanted us to know about him.

"I am retired from the army. I bought this small shop to have something to do." The shopkeeper briefly hesitated and appeared to be gathering his thoughts. "I like a small town. It reminds me of the one I grew up in as a child. I was the youngest of twelve children. How many children do you have?"

"We have five children," Helen responded. At that moment, I realized that my wife didn't say seven children because she didn't want to have to explain the tragic loss of two of our children.

"Not even people in eastern Turkey have large families anymore. It's expensive isn't it?" he asked.

"Yes. But I love children," Helen said.

The shopkeeper rose and put his arm around Helen and then hugged me. "Would you like another cup of tea?" the shopkeeper asked.

"Afraid I've had my limit for the morning," I said, as the shopkeeper laughed.

"So ... how much do you want for the camel saddles?" I asked.

"Well, you're not really a tourist, and you do live here. I'll give you a good deal. You can have the both for one hundred Turkish lira."

"That is a good price, but will you take ninety?" I asked. I could tell the shop-keeper was thinking of what to say next.

"Sure, why not?" he said.

We were now the proud owners of not one, but two, camel saddles, one for each of us. They appeared to be made from old kilim carpets whose owners were happy to find some final use for them. One village specialized in making these saddles for the purpose of selling them to tourists. No Turkish camel owner would have considered purchasing any one of these saddles with the intention of using it to ride his camel.

The shopkeeper, speaking limited English, asked Helen her name.

"I'm Helen, from America," she responded.

The shopkeeper, looking at me, asked, "What's your name?"

"I'm Ed," I responded.

The shopkeeper's face lit up. "Ahmed! From America!" he said.

Looking confused, I said, "No! I'm Ed."

"Yes! Ahmed," he said.

Realizing further explanation was useless, I became Ahmed on that day. I'm now referred to as *Ahmed from America* in the local shops and restaurants in our village.

CHAPTER 1

▼

ONE WORLD

There are no boundaries between countries when the earth is seen from space; it's one earth and one people. Traveling to the places that everyone tells me I shouldn't go has opened my mind to distant horizons. From 1985 until 2001 I traveled the world on business, meeting successful businessmen and women in Asia, Africa, and Europe. In no way did this prepare me for visiting these same places years later on my own. When traveling on my own, I didn't stay at five-star hotels, eat at fine dining establishments, and negotiate and interact with the countries' privileged and elite. Immediately following my retirement in 2001, I circumnavigated the world aboard my sailboat. I've traveled to places so remote they see few, if any, outsiders.

In countries presented to us in the West as enemies of our way of life, I have discovered their governments don't represent the average people, who want only safety and security for themselves and their children. News reported to Americans by the major news networks and papers doesn't always match the everyday reality I've found in these places. It's not fair to say that all news reported is inaccurate, but there are different ways of emphasizing news content, and this can contribute to misunderstanding.

An example of this was the 2004 tsunami in Thailand. After weeks of hearing about the coastal destruction of major Thailand tourist resorts, tourists in large numbers cancelled their plans to travel to this beautiful country. Many Thais lost their jobs and the ability to support their families with the meager income they had been earning. The reality is that less than 10 percent of the tourist areas in Thailand were affected, but because of the emphasis on reporting bad news, the impact on Thailand was much worse than it had to be. Expanding upon this, I've come to believe that because of the way in which news is often reported, people sometimes believe we have political enemies that don't exist.

Away from the States, our sailing base of operations is Turkey. Each day I meet German, English, Scandinavian, French, Israeli, and Turkish sailors in the marina. I'm always interested in what these people think of the United States. Again and again, I hear alienation and resentment toward the United States government for a multitude of reasons—most involving the invasion of Iraq and widespread concern that Europe is being pulled into a disastrous and, at best, dubious future. Europeans feel vulnerable to terrorism and clearly understand this growing threat on their soil; some blame the United States for this recent vulnerability.

In contrast, I believe it's been difficult for Americans to experience this vulnerability, which has been thrust upon them only recently. In some ways, 9/11 was America's loss of innocence and awakening to what most of the world has experienced throughout history. A question we must all ask ourselves is: *How is America coping with this new threat, and how are we being influenced away from an opportunity of peacemaking and globalization?*

Helen and I sailed to Turkey three years ago and have chosen to remain here because the lifestyle suits us. During the first two years, we lived aboard *Tahlequah*, and we purchased a home here during the third year. We haven't ceased to be Americans but have instead been broadened by our exposure to other peoples and cultures. Living in Turkey, a Muslim country, has contributed to altering my perceptions of what life is like living outside the United States. Turkey is both European and Asian, occupying two continents. Our home is located in a small Turkish village and our time is divided between sailing the Mediterranean and living in our home. It's a life that we enjoy. Although there are opportunities for improvement, Turkey embraces many democratic values and principles I took for granted in the United States.

We have installed a satellite dish on our roof and are able to watch the U.S. news, as well as European and Asian networks. This provides a balanced view of world news events from varying perspectives. I was able to compare Western views with those of the rest of the world. Although I've always known that by listening to others we can learn more about ourselves, putting this into practice can require great effort.

One example of promulgated misunderstanding was an article that we received in our e-mail from a person claiming to be a retired senior officer in the U.S. Air Force. Its purpose was to convince people to support the war in Iraq and what he considered to be traditional patriotic American values.

The author attempted to justify racial profiling, stating, "You can't name one Muslim country there is freedom of speech, women are equal, and is a democracy."

There were countless inaccuracies that attacked the very core of what Turkey stands for. The unfortunate part is that many Americans have little or no knowledge of life in other countries, including Muslim ones. My purpose in writing this book is to help to find common denominators between Westerners and other people throughout the world.

Just before we made final arrangements to travel to eastern Turkey, three bombs exploded in the nearby tourist town of Marmaris. These bombings were reportedly carried out by the PKK, an outlawed terrorist group fighting for the creation of a Kurdish state in eastern Turkey. They are accused of many previous bombings in Turkey. Although sixteen people were injured on this occasion, there were fortunately no fatalities. Few tourists travel to eastern Turkey because of the fear of terrorism resulting from Kurdish separatists crossing into Turkey from Iraq. The PKK is to Turkey what Al-Qaeda is to the United States. For years this conflict has endured, and even today there is threat of a Turkish incursion into Iraq to rout out the three thousand suspected PKK terrorists hiding out in the mountains.

The PKK is a small minority of the Kurdish population of thirty million people. The Kurds are the largest ethnic minority in the world without a homeland. Although they have been temporarily designated small states by major world powers, they were abandoned by those supporting them, for many reasons, and in the long term they are unable to defend and maintain these homelands.

My first challenge when planning our trip was to locate a tour company willing to take us to this remote region in spite of recent terrorist activities. Mentioning eastern Turkey brought the same result: silence. Researching old travel brochures, we learned of an Australian company that had specialized in these tours in years past. Unfortunately, we were unable to locate any recent reference to them on the Internet. Following our fruitless attempts, our good friend Tolga, of Akustik Travel in Bodrum, volunteered to help us. A week later, we received a phone call informing us he had located a company. They conducted this tour only once a year, and had many people committed, mostly Australians. As time passed, we learned that most had cancelled, with the exception of two Australian women. Apparently, the tourists were frightened by recent bombings.

Mentioning our intended visit to eastern Turkey always brought the same response: "Don't go there!" We heard this repeatedly. We received the same advice from family and friends back in the United States and from many of our Turkish friends.

When we challenged them to say why we shouldn't go there, we were told, "It's too dangerous; you could be killed. No one goes there."

We received an e-mail from a cousin of Helen's, whom we hold in high regard and respect. His experience in traveling and background provide realistic insights into the lifestyle we've chosen to lead. He wrote:

After your last update I considered writing back immediately to caution your movements in and around Turkey, Lebanon, and Israel, as you'd mentioned. This most recent threat issued by Islamic extremists should, if it hasn't already, cause you to carefully rethink your plans—at least for now. You have enjoyed freedoms few others have, and nothing would please me more than for you to complete your plans to roam through all that history—but these guys are completely nuts, and there is need for caution the likes of which we haven't seen recently.

His words were precise, and his warning represented a sound and reasonable view in today's confused world.

It's difficult to put into words why we've chosen to lead this kind of life. Sailing around the world is in itself fraught with dangers, as we now well know. We didn't do it because it was dangerous, but we accepted the dangers that came with fulfilling a dream. My closest friend, a big-game hunter, stands in front of a charging elephant, lion, leopard, or polar bear several times a year, knowing better than most that if he were to make one mistake, he would die. He doesn't do it because it's dangerous; he does it because it's his dream to live the experience.

We knew if we found ourselves in danger, it wouldn't be the first time. During our circumnavigation, we had one incident off the coast of the Hamish Islands in Yemen. Our rudder steering broken, and in 70-knot winds, we made the decision to seek refuge in a remote bay in Yemen to make the necessary repairs. Although we had been given warning not to stop there under any circumstances, we felt we had no choice.

Suddenly, we found ourselves being circled by a speed boat carrying ten men with automatic weapons, many of which appeared to be pointing at us. After circling us several times and seeing we were having a lot of difficulty, they waved us toward shore and left. Although we never knew who these men were, we preferred to believe they were military, in spite of the fact they wore no uniforms.

On another occasion we had to make an emergency stop on a remote island in Indonesia because there was no wind, and, even worse, we were low on fuel. Again, we were warned not to stop there because of anti-foreigner sentiments and their association with Bali terrorism. An Australian yacht arrived with us, and we anchored and went ashore with our diesel cans in search of fuel.

Seeing us, a man with a motorcycle came to offer a ride into town for fuel. He invited us into what can only be described as a cage attached to the back of his motorcycle. We jumped in, and the man swung the cage gate shut. Hearing the latch lock behind us didn't provide us with a warm, fuzzy feeling.

As we were driving through the center of town, our driver began to yell in English, "I have an American! I have an Australian!"

Hearing this, people, including children, came running toward us from all directions. Fearing the worst, Peter and I looked at one another despairingly, as if to say, *What in the hell did we get ourselves into now?* Unexpectedly, people began to talk to us using the few English words they knew. Apparently, visitors to their island were rare, and we were to be given the same welcome the royal family might expect.

Because it was Ramadan, no water or food could be eaten before sunset. We were taken to a private home. Once we were inside, the shutters were closed, and we were offered food and a bottle of coke. The family proceeded to put on a Michael Jackson rock video, believing that we would feel at home. Surprisingly, the children spoke a little English, and they proceeded to ask us many questions about America and Australia. They took great interest in everything we said, until finally we had to explain that our wives were still on the boat, and we would have to return.

Visiting the site of the Bali nightclub bomb blast in Indonesia and Bali Peace Park across the street was a sad, sobering, and inspiring experience. Loved ones, friends, and others would visit, continuously leaving on the fence surrounding the site inspirational poems, writings, and symbols of this tragic loss. The many names and countries of the victims are inscribed on a marble monument across the street. After reading the many personal messages left at the fence and written on a banner, it was difficult to leave without fighting back tears.

Some of these innocent victims were themselves Muslim and Hindu. Traveling through Indonesia, I heard nothing but anger against those who perpetrated this crime against humanity. Everywhere I've traveled, I've encountered people who want peace for their families and their countries.

In the weeks before leaving for eastern Turkey, we spoke openly with our good friends Tolga and Uri, both of whom were knowledgeable and in a position to caution us. Both assured us we would be safe and that we would see another side of Turkey few tourists experienced and one we wouldn't forget. When I asked Uri if he would take responsibility for our ransom should we be abducted, he assured me he would pay Helen's. *Well*, I thought, *half our problem is solved.* Although many attempted to dissuade us from venturing to eastern Turkey, I'd made my decision. I've said many times I'd rather be lucky than smart, and, by God, I've been lucky in life.

For centuries, Greeks and Turks shared common shores without the strict boundaries created by governments in recent times. It's not uncommon to see the ruins of Greek villages with Roman architectural influence found throughout Turkey. Turkey is a modern country rich in its heritage. Because Turkey separates Asia from Europe, it's tolerant and accepting of all cultures. In Turkey, Christians, Jews, and Muslims live together peacefully and have for centuries. At one time, Turkey sent its naval forces offshore of Spain demanding that persecuted Jews be allowed to board Turkish ships, from where they would be taken to safe haven in Turkey. Over three hundred thousand Jews voluntarily left Spain for Turkey during the height of the Inquisition. Even today Jews live in Turkey. The Ottoman Empire ruled much of the Mediterranean and the Middle East for almost six hundred years and until the end of World War I. To do this successfully, they insisted upon the peaceful coexistence of all people under their influence and offered equal protection to everyone. It was only after this period, and the dissolution of the Ottoman Empire, that the Arabs, Greeks, Russians, Armenians, and Turks began to fight one another.

Much, if not all, of this conflict was propagated by the Western alliance post-World War I in an effort to divide the spoils of the Ottoman Empire amongst themselves. For centuries, and up until World War I, European powers had been unsuccessful at controlling the Middle East. Promoting new states with governments appointed by the Western powers gave them for the first time the opportunity to influence and control these faraway lands rich in oil. By dividing what had once been one empire, the Western powers succeeded in promoting conflict that resulted in war between peoples who had lived together peacefully for centuries. Today, even after so many decades, the sad Armenian issue looms over Turkey, still unresolved.

The formation of the Republic of Turkey after World War I was spearheaded by the great leader Mustafa Kemal Ataturk, who was intent on bringing democracy to Turkey. His contributions were many, including instituting a civil penal system modeled on Swiss and Germanic penal codes, ending polygamy, adapting surnames for his people, separating religion and politics, and modeling the republic on European values and standards without abandoning Turkish culture. Ataturk was intent on moving Turkey away from identification with the Middle East and realigning it with European values. A major step for Turkey was to separate church and state, resulting in the creation of a constitutionally formed secular state. The Turkish army sees itself charged with the responsibility of ensuring that the constitution is not violated, and it has on more than one occasion removed elected government officials because of assumed constitutional violations. The European Union continues to demand that the Turkish military separate itself from the political process as a requirement for entry into that union.

A concern today among Turkish secularists is the growing political support and election of nonsecularists. Although these individuals have sworn allegiance to the Turkish constitution and a secularist state, nevertheless, many oppose nonsecularists in fear that they will make future changes to the constitution. One fundamental concern among secularists is the threat that the constitution might be amended to permit the wearing of headscarves in public buildings. As Westerners, we take for granted the freedom of religious expression. To many Westerners, the wearing of headscarves would not in itself be an issue. I suspect that because Turkey is bordered by Islamic fundamentalist countries, who are accused of sponsoring extremism and terrorism, this tends to be a major issue. Although I see no indication that Turkey will become an Islamic fundamentalist state, the fear that the country could move in that direction is a divisive issue among Turkey's citizens today. There have been mass peaceful rallies and demonstrations in the streets involving over a million people showing support for secularism.

I looked upon this trip as a training opportunity and hoped to learn from it. Next, I'd planned to travel to other Middle Eastern countries known for their perceived hostilities toward Westerners. Whatever the risk, I needed to learn the truth.

From reading about Muslims and talking with Muslim-Turkish friends, I discovered that Christians and Muslims have grounds for a common understanding. Although Muslims are aware of our common shared beliefs, many Christians are unaware of them. I, myself, was surprised to discover that Muslims accept the virgin birth and all of the prophets, including Abraham and Moses, and that they accept Jesus as a prophet. Today, the body of John the Baptist is enshrined in a mosque.

Many Westerners are unaware that the Virgin Mary, St. Paul, and the earliest Christians lived in what today is Turkey. The earliest Christian towns were first established here in Turkey. The crusaders found friendly villages whose residents were accepting and tolerant. These same crusaders laid siege to villages, including Constantinople (now Istanbul). The early Christian communities in Turkey refused to support European crusaders, choosing instead to live in harmony with their Muslim neighbors. When the crusaders surrendered under siege, the Muslim armies granted them freedom of passage to return home, under oath that they would never return.

The Turkish and Middle Eastern Islamic cultures are different from Western culture. This first became evident to us when we rode public buses. Men and children, almost without exception, will offer their seats to all women, regardless of age.

While at the marina where we berth our sailboat, *Tahlequah*, we noticed European children and Turkish children swimming together in the pool. We saw European children yelling and screaming, diving from the restaurant side of the pool, getting people wet, throwing things, ignoring their protesting parents, and sometimes cursing. By contrast, we noticed that, almost without exception, the Turkish children were well behaved, disciplined, and accepted instruction from adults. Cursing among Muslim children, young adults, and others is almost unheard of. Walking on the streets here is considered safe during the day and at night. The village accepts responsibility for correcting an out-of-control youth. Helen has never removed her jewelry or diamond rings when traveling in Turkey, something she feels forced to do in some countries.

Chapter 2

▼

The People of Eastern Turkey

We had long ago accepted the fact that not all places could be visited by yacht. There were often times when it was necessary to leave *Tahlequah* in the safety of a marina, where she would be cared for while we toured the interior of the country. Doing this with some frequency allowed us to see more of a country, enjoying the sights, sounds, and culture these places had to offer.

Reviewing our eastern Turkey itinerary, I was excited that we would travel by land from Adana, near the Mediterranean Sea, eastward along the Syrian border to the towns of Antakya, Gaza Anter, Sanliurea, Mardin, and Batman, then travel northeastward along the border of Iran and the cities of Bitlis, Van, and Agri. Then we would travel northward toward the Black Sea and cities of Agri, Kars, Artvin, Rize, and finally Trabzon, where we would get a flight back to Istanbul. On occasion we would be within one or more kilometers of the Syrian, Iraqi, and Iranian borders. Uri informed me that we would be safe here, because the Turkish army presence was established in these areas.

The morning before leaving on our eastern Turkey adventure, I climbed *Tahlequah*'s mast to perform some necessary task. Descending to the deck, I experienced a terrible pain in my lower spine and stumbled below, in anguish with the pain. Helen asked if I needed help.

"Just call a doctor," I responded.

"Are you injured?" Helen asked, concerned that I was in a serious way.

"I'm not sure, but I am sure he'll have to come and give me a painkiller. I'll be okay," I said, half believing my own words.

"I'll be back in ten minutes," Helen said, as she whisked up the entryway and onto the dock.

Helen returned a short time later bearing news that the doctor was on his way to *Tahlequah*. Within ten minutes, we heard a knocking on the hull; the doctor had arrived. After I explained my situation and that I would be leaving within hours for eastern Turkey, the doctor gave me a shot, with the promise that everything would be okay. He provided Helen with a syringe, additional dose, and a prescription to bring with us in the event the pain continued.

Two hours later, I was walking, getting dressed, and passing duffel bags onto the dock. Fearing a setback, I called my friend Tolga, who had provided me with a rental car, and requested that he send someone to drive us to the airport. When the driver arrived, he brought to my attention the missing front license plate. Knowing it had been on the car when it was rented, I could offer no explanation. I later learned that someone had found the license plate on the road and mailed it back to Akustik Travel, whose name was on the plate.

Only in Turkey, I thought to myself.

The day had arrived: we were ready to travel to eastern Turkey, the land of mystery. Following a one-hour flight to Istanbul and a quick change of planes, we were headed to the city of Adana, population two million people. We took a cab to the Surmel Hotel in the downtown area. Because it was late at night, we had to replace dinner with a simple cup of coffee.

The next morning, we awoke early, made our way to the dining room to discover many empty tables with signs reserving them for occupants who would never arrive, due to mass cancellations. Not sure of our tour company name, we surveyed the tables. We had to choose between one sign saying Climax Tours, and a second sign saying Age Tours. As we began to sit at the Climax table, our guide, Anna, arrived, shepherding us to the table saying Age Tours. We made the best of our situation, introduced ourselves, and discovered that *Age* was an abbreviation for Aegean Tours, a great relief to us all. I later learned that the Climax tour had been cancelled.

It was at breakfast that we met our fellow adventurers for the first time. Elise, along with her husband, owned a successful farming operation in Australia. Her husband encouraged her to pursue her hobby of traveling throughout the world, while he ran their farming operation. Our other Australian adventurer was Glenda, a single nurse who also enjoyed traveling to far-off places in every corner of the world. Both women had traveled together in the past and appeared to get along well.

Anna, our guide, was an independent, modern-thinking Turkish woman in her early thirties. She chose to follow the Hindu religion after having made many pilgrimages to India. Before becoming a tour guide, she had been a diamond merchant. Over the next several days, we learned about Anna and how her modern ways were sometimes in conflict with her family's values. Anna typically joined us for dinner, afterward retiring early to perform yoga exercises and meditate.

Leaving Adana, we traveled to the city of Antakya, formerly Antioch, one of sixty-nine cities established by Alexander the Great and named for his father. Antakya is a bustling city with a population of a quarter of a million people. There are ancient as well as modern streets with old homes and storefronts. Jews, Christians, Muslims, artists, writers, and wealthy merchants lived here during the seventh century. Here we explored the largest mosaic museum in Turkey and the Cave of Peter, where the name *Christian* first appears in writings. We saw in the Muze Giril Bileti (tile museum) beautiful wall and floor mosaics with amazing detail.

Having lunch in a second-story building, we heard traditional music coming from below. Someone was loudly playing a drum and flutes in the street next to a humble dwelling. We were informed by our guide that it was likely a young man entering the military to perform his mandatory service. The music was typically Kurdish: melodic and captivating. It appeared to be a time of celebration; everyone was enjoying themselves as the young man looked out the window and waved to the musicians below. The music attracted many onlookers who gathered below the window to clap with the music.

I was aware that every young man in Turkey was required to perform military service as a part of his civic responsibility, and this young man was likely being drafted into one of the military services. I asked Anna to call the man in the window and invite him to join us. Reluctantly, Anna cooperated, and the young man came to meet us. Through Anna, I asked him if he were entering the military.

"Yes," said the young man.

"Does that frighten you?" I asked.

"My father served in the military, and my grandfather fought for the Republic." The young man said this proudly.

"Do you have reservations about entering the military?" I asked, and Anna translated my words almost simultaneously.

"Oh, no. Everyone has to do it," the young man said. Just then, someone from upstairs called to him.

"I have to help my brother."

After I thanked him for taking the time to speak to me, we left to return to our minivan, as he hurriedly disappeared into the house.

Driving to the city of Gaziantep, we were suddenly stopped by plainclothes police or military, we never established which. Opening the rear door of our minivan, they appeared satisfied with its contents. Although tourists were uncommon in this area, it was clear we were tourists and posed no threat.

The city of Gaziantep is entirely Kurdish and has a population of one million people. After checking in to the Ravanda Hotel, we walked the city streets. We received many surprised, but friendly, stares. Shopkeepers didn't bargain here and made no special effort to entice us into their shops. Entering a shop, it wasn't difficult to find a shopkeeper who spoke some English, at least enough to understand us.

Informing the desk clerk back at the hotel that we wished to experience a *hamam* (Turkish bath), we at first received only a blank stare, as if to say, *You what?* He did arrange for a cab to take us to a local hamam.

The bath area was constructed of marble, with a high, domed ceiling, much like a mosque. In the center of the room was a large raised, heated marble table. Given a *pasha* (towel), we were each invited to lie on a heated marble table to relax the muscles. Three Turkish men bathed and massaged me, while three women did the same to Helen. Our skin was exfoliated using coarse goatskin mittens. We were told that because this was a coed hamam, Turkish women will not work here. Instead, Russian women cater to the women. In traditional hamam, men and women are kept apart either by separate facilities or a dedicated schedule. The bathing and exfoliation process using the goatskin mitten can be compared to a healthy sanding.

Following this, we were lathered beneath a voluminous mountain of soapsuds, and massaged. After failing to close my mouth, I began spitting soap suds. Buckets of warm water were brought to wash away the soap, one of which was poured over my head. Cleansed of all impurities, one can leave or stay for further massage. The process of cleansing one's body is a Muslim custom. All mosques have outside places to sit and wash one's hands, feet, and face prior to entering to pray. Afterward, we were wrapped in towels and invited to sit in a special area and served Turkish tea. The total cost was US$12.

Washing and cleanliness are taken for granted today. During the time of the crusades, even knights rarely bathed, and they used their clothing for a multitude of purposes. Because they used the same soiled clothing during the day and night, this frequently gave rise to health issues. By contrast, Muslims had strict bathing practices. Hamans were provided for the average population as well as the wealthy. It's important to understand that during the period leading up to the crusades, and for many centuries before, while Europe was in the throes of the Dark Ages, Muslim artists, mathematicians, astronomers, and even scholars became repositories for the preservation of scholarly knowledge and the arts.

Leaving the hamam, we decided to walk back to the hotel instead of taking a cab. Running through the streets, young boys were transporting Turkish tea on trays to shopkeepers. We've observed these trays being spun overhead without the loss of a glass. Shopkeepers sitting outside encourage passersby to enter their shops; some, but not all, speak English. Entering a shop, one is offered Turkish tea or coffee, and refusing is a sign of poor taste. Turkish coffee is very strong; the bottom third cannot be consumed due to its syrupy consistency and strong, bitter taste. Unable to develop the fine art of knowing when to stop, I often made the mistake of swallowing the thick syrup at the bottom of the cup. The sudden expression on my face would say it all.

Because it was still early in the evening, I approached the desk clerk after arriving back at the hotel. Wanting to experience a whirling dervish ceremony, I asked if this could be arranged. Consulting his watch and offering to call us a cab, he said I could still make it if I hurried, so we were soon off to hear Sufi music and see a whirling dervish ceremony. Before we left the hotel, the desk clerk handed me a brochure in English that explained both the ceremony and who the dervishes were.

I discovered that the dervishes are interesting and remarkable people who are ascetic Muslim monks. These are Muslims who freely give of their possessions to the less fortunate. They are pacifists who historically gave sanctuary to soldiers, indifferent to nationality within their monasteries. Dervishes are a universal sect, not limited to Turkey. Today, many young Muslims in Iran have joined the dervishes as a means of expressing their independence of the existing political oligarchy. The whirling dervish ceremony is foremost a religious ceremony. The dervishes remove their cloaks and begin whirling in rhythm to the music of a flute and drum, as chanters give praise to God. Their long white robes extend to the floor, giving a floating appearance to their motions.

Just as the moon and planets revolve on their own axes around the sun, the dervishes revolve around the room. Dervishes believe whirling is a means to reach divine reality, an intoxication of the soul. As their faces evolve into a trancelike state, they seem to accomplish the physically impossible. Their whirling becomes faster and faster, their long white robes twirling high into the air, creating a breeze within the room, as they spin in harmonious circles. One hand is slowly elevated upward and the other downward, symbolizing that from God we receive, to man we give—we keep nothing to ourselves.

How it's possible to spin at these speeds in perfect harmony, without becoming dizzy and falling down, defies our imaginations. It's a remarkable combination of skill and faith. The whirling is repeated several times at increasing speeds to the accompaniment of Sufi music and chanting. The music is tranquilizing and hypnotic, perfect for this ceremony. As observers, we are left with the feeling we've witnessed something great, the spiritual essence and elevation of man.

As we left Antioch, the topography changed dramatically; we saw miles and miles of pistachio trees, another major crop in Turkey. We crossed the Euphrates River, which flows through Turkey to the Persian Gulf before it joins the Tigris. We passed the Karabrun Halfeti Dam, constructed for both irrigation and hydro-electric power in the 1990s. I commented that I was surprised to see no visible sign of security at the dam. Looking bewildered, Anna asked why anyone would need security at a dam. I responded that in the United States all dams and power plants are protected, because they are considered potential prime targets of terrorists. Anna gave me a surprised look that confirmed her confusion at my point.

"Well, we don't have to worry about things like that here," Anna said confidently.

Visible nearby was a beautiful castle built in the eleventh or twelfth century. Unlike what we were used to on the Aegean and Mediterranean coasts, all women in the nearby village wore Muslim clothing (burkas). Their clothing didn't inhibit them from saying Gunaydin (good morning) as they passed us.

Parking the minivan, we walked across an ancient Roman bridge to a small village. Anna informed us that this village was scheduled to be flooded as a result of the planned construction of a new watershed and dam. Apparently local newspapers were protesting the loss of this beautiful village and surrounding countryside. No one was sure what would happen. Helen and her friend Elise noticed a group of athletic young men, wearing similar shorts and parkas, sitting in front of a small shop, drinking tea. We sat on very small stools next to them and ordered tea. Everyone began talking English; they identified themselves as the number-two Turkish professional football (soccer) team, en route to a major playoff. Helen and Elise requested to have their pictures taken with the team; they were more than happy to accommodate and appeared to enjoy our company.

Following a brief boat ride on a local lake, we proceeded to enjoy a fresh fish lunch in a local outdoor restaurant. Only one item was on the menu: the only type of fish found in the lake, accompanied by homemade village bread baked in a wood-burning oven. The meal was delicious. At first, I felt sorry for our guide, Anna, because she was a strict vegetarian, refusing to eat both fish and chicken. She did impose on the owner to prepare her a vegetable dish, consisting of potatoes and carrots. Then we were off to the Harran Hotel, which reminded me of an old Hilton, with beautiful large rooms. En route from the lobby to our room, the elevator became stuck between floors. Following a half hour of hollering, we ultimately attracted the attention of a porter who assisted us in soliciting additional help. I suppose our frantic behavior overcame the language difficulties. Eventually, we reached our room with luggage in hand, no worse for wear and tear.

As we traveled eastward through Turkey, it was obvious the people were poorer, and the topography arid and comparable to the outback of Australia. Many people living in eastern Turkey are of Kurdish or Arabic descent and dress differently from those elsewhere in Turkey. There are many farms here; the average farm laborer earns US$2,200 annually. The farmlands are vast and extensive with adobe/mud homes of simple construction. The Turkish government has begun to upgrade the infrastructure, including roads, hospitals, and schools. After the first few days of traveling through local villages, I realized concerns for our safety were unfounded.

I intended to take every advantage of the fact that we were a small tour and could easily deviate from the routine major attractions in favor of going to out-of-the-way places and meeting everyday people. This would be my opportunity to meet, talk to, and interview people.

We drove forty kilometers to the town of Harran to see their beehive houses. These houses are constructed of bricks gathered from local ancient ruins, bonded using a mixture of mud and straw. Having cone-shaped domes erected over square-shaped houses made these structures distinctive and unusual. Internal arches supported these domes, with vents in the center to promote the escape of heat and smoke. Every three years, the inhabitants recoated the interior walls with a mortarlike substance to reinforce the structure.

I asked Anna to locate a family we could visit and, more importantly, spend time with discussing life in the village. We were invited into one large beehive house consisting of several attached buildings with beehive dome ceilings. The owner's name was Halil, and he was dressed in Arabic clothing. He was a tall, thin man with a graying mustache. Inside his home were many Turkish carpets scattered about with pillows. He had eleven children and one wife. The children were playing a board game similar to one we saw in South Africa played by the Zulus. His children spoke English. One of the older children informed me there were enough children in their family to form one football (soccer) team, and frequently they competed against other local teams.

We stayed for tea and enjoyed sitting on camel saddles. Halil's family had lived in this house for nineteen generations. They spoke both Arabic and Turkish. Halil was a soft-spoken man appearing to be gentle and understanding of his wife and children. Outside in the yard was a swing and cradle used to mix yogurt and a horse-drawn cart for transportation. We saw raised platforms constructed for the family to sleep outside. Sleeping outside is common in this area and a means of escaping the summer's heat. Kerosene-filled saucers are placed beneath the platform legs to discourage scorpions from threatening occupants.

"What countries are you from?" Halil asked through our translator.

"I'm from America," I said.

"We don't see Americans here. It is good you have come. You are our guest."

"I appreciate your agreeing to let us see your home and spend time with you here. What is life like here in your village?" I asked.

"I would not want to live anywhere else; we have always lived here," Halil said.

"How about your older children? Are they happy here in the village?"

"Life is different today than when I was a child living here in this house. Everything is different today." He said this squinting and rolling his eyes as if to suggest he wasn't pleased.

"How is it different today?" I asked.

"Children today expect more. They want more, and they're never satisfied, just being here like we were when I was a child growing up. I didn't expect anything; there were too many children. I knew better than to ask for things I knew I couldn't have. Today it's different, very different. It's harder today growing up now."

While touring, we encountered a large group of American archeologists who were also exploring the ruins and culture of eastern Turkey. We were informed they were reviewing several archeological sites for the purpose of prioritizing future archeological projects to be funded by American universities. Although academics, they appeared to be like any other group of tourists.

A short walk from the village, we climbed a steep hill and entered an old castle, the Harran Kalesi Castle. Although the exact date is unknown, it is believed the castle was restored by local rulers in 1059. Two young men speaking English offered to give us a tour of the ruin. The castle was massive, as are most in Turkey. There were many cavernous rooms, including a hamam for both men and women.

Four preadolescent girls followed us in an effort to sell us necklaces made of seeds, which were guaranteed to ward off mosquitoes. The young men ushered the young girls away. They became more clever and pursued us from within the castle corridors, hiding as they went. Before leaving, we purchased several of these mosquito-preventing beads from the girls. As we left the village, we donated pencils, erasers, and crayons to the children.

Leaving the village, we saw a very poor school, with children playing in the schoolyard. Because we had previously purchased school supplies for distribution in eastern Turkey, we stopped. Anna spoke with the teacher in charge and soon motioned for us to follow her into the school. The teacher was a young man in his early twenties, dressed in a suit with tie. He was grateful for our donation of supplies and invited us into the classroom to meet his students. Because there was only one classroom, children ranging in age from seven through fourteen sat together. Some of the older students appeared to be helping younger ones with their studies. The children took great interest in us and proceeded to practice the few English words they knew. Someone would say hello, and when we responded "hello," everyone would cheer. When the teacher explained to his students that we were from America and Australia, they seemed amazed we would come so far just to visit them—a myth we chose not to dispel. Further discussion led to our understanding what other supplies the children lacked. Pooling our money together, we made a small financial donation for paint to cover the schoolrooms. The children sensed that their teacher approved of our visit, and they responded in kind.

As we left, the children began screaming, "Come back, Americans! Come back Australians!" As we were driving down the dirt road leaving the village, a man stopped his tractor, stood, and waved to us.

I was relieved that I was able to continue my journey without any recurring back problems.

CHAPTER 3

▼

LIVING TOGETHER

In every village, town, and city, we heard the call to prayer five times a day, beginning at dawn, then again at midday, midafternoon, sunset, and just prior to the end of day. Although prayers are spoken in Arabic, most people do not speak or understand Arabic; it's comparable to the use of Latin in Christianity. When translated, the words calling the faithful to prayer are:

There is only one God
Mohammed is his messenger
Come to pray
Come to salvation
Come to felicity

We visited the city of prophets, the city of Urfa, where the prophet Abraham was born and lived in a cave until he was seven years old. Washing in a natural spring inside this cave is believed to help cure diseases, similar to Lourdes. On the spot where King Nemrod ordered Abraham to be burned alive, the story says, the fire turned to water and the burning logs to fish; these were surrounded by a pleasant rose garden. Today, there are two beautiful lakes filled with carp, purportedly created from the burning logs. We purchased dishes of flakes and fed the carp, as did many children. The water seemed alive with fish as they leaped into the air for food. It's a quiet, tranquil, and beautiful place, surrounded by white limestone structures, including a beautiful mosque.

We removed our shoes and entered the cave where Abraham was born. It was obvious to us that this was a special place where fathers brought their sons and mothers brought their daughters; there was a separate entrance for men and women. Families came here to walk the grounds and enjoy the beautiful, peaceful surroundings. As we walked the narrow walkway surrounding the small lake, men and women dressed in traditional Muslim clothing held the hands of their young children and smiled as they passed us. Young lovers walked hand in hand, unaware of us and intent only upon one another. The tombs of Job, his wife, and Elijah are in the nearby village of Urfa. People outside the cave stopped to have their pictures taken as a souvenir of their visit. A man was providing colorful robes to both men and women alike. Helen, Elise, and Glenda put on long robes and headcovers.

A young man from a local university joined the women to have his picture taken with them. Upon learning Helen was American, he took a special interest and began asking her questions about America. After answering his questions, Helen began to ask a few of her own. We did learn from him that his dreams and ambitions in life were no different than those of any American. He wanted to make his parents proud of him, to be successful in life, and to one day have a family of his own. There could be no doubt that the families who had come here today were happy to share this beautiful and tranquil place with us. The atmosphere was alive and exciting, and although there were few outsiders visiting this sacred shrine, everyone made us feel welcome.

When we arrived at our hotel, we noticed an American flag had been raised in our honor. My initial reaction was one of concern. I asked Anna if it was safe to advertise that Helen and I were Americans. Anna wasted no time in responding, "Why not? Americans are welcome here." I was reassured that recent terrorist activities were not directed toward foreigners, and Americans were especially safe. This was not the impression I'd gotten from television back home. Anna also stressed that Kurds here were Turkish and we should not think they were all terrorists. She differentiated between the PKK, a terrorist group funded and supported by some Kurds wanting to establish a separate state, and the many others who had been living peacefully in Turkey for many generations.

After leaving the hotel, we made a one-hour drive to Mount Nemrud, a most mysterious place, second only to the pyramids of Egypt. We took special notice of farmers riding tractors, in some cases accompanied by their wives wearing headscarves. When we waved at field workers, they always returned the wave.

The ascending roadway was narrow, steep, and had many vertical drop-offs into deep gorges. Mount Nemrud is 2,150 meters high, and the goliath ten-meter-high statues at the top were created by the Kommagene civilization. The unique art discovered at the top of Mount Nemrud became the synthesis of later Persian and Greek arts. Antiochus's sacred tomb at the top of Mount Nemrud is buried beneath sixty meters of rubble, making excavation difficult, if not impossible, even with today's technology. It is considered the eighth wonder of the world. The temperature at the top was much cooler, and the brisk prevailing wind quickly chilled us.

Helen and I had great difficulty walking to the top because of the rocky terrain. Once there, we circled both the east and west terraces; the goliath statues were breathtaking. They were scattered in close proximity to their original resting places. The heads were so large that it's difficult to imagine how they were erected with the technology of the time. Heads of the king himself, his wife, lion, and eagle were all present in their full splendor beneath the tomb of the king. Many inscriptions upon stone blocks detailed the meaning and civilization of this remarkable site and period. We ended our perfect day by watching the sun descend upon the horizon from the top of Mount Nemrud.

The following morning, we drove one hour to the Siverek Lake and dam. Awaiting the arrival of the ferry, we enjoyed a cup of tea at a nearby outdoor restaurant situated along the water's edge. Below us, we observed women wearing burkas, beating their wash on rocks. Within the restaurant, men and women sat separately, seemingly ignoring one another. As the ferry approached the dock, everyone gathered for boarding. After the arriving people disembarked, we boarded along with local people carrying bags of goods for trading and sale, some balancing these on their heads. The ferry appeared to have enjoyed many years of good service and was now in need of repairs and a coat of fresh paint to hide its rusting metal boilerplate sides. Boarding the ferry, I took notice that there were no visible life jackets or emergency life rafts.

Moving to the top deck, we observed the people below. Two drivers from an old diesel truck began dancing to the Kurdish music coming from their truck radio, as people watched and clapped to the music. Several young girls, aged eleven to fourteen, attempted to talk to us, while the older women ignored our presence. A few of them wore colorful headscarves, and all wore long, patterned skirts. We learned that the girls came to this area for the purpose of collecting hazelnuts and were returning to the city with their harvest in burlap bags.

Throughout our hour-long river journey, they asked many questions, including where we were from, what it was like, how we were enjoying Turkey, and what kind of music we listened to. Except for their dress, these children were no different from those back home, inquisitive and friendly. They seemed thrilled that we had come from so far away, and we couldn't help but enjoy their company.

I asked, "What do you think of America?"

"We like America," one of the young girls responded.

"And why do you like America?" I asked.

"They have nice clothes," another young girl responded. "Good music, too," another said.

Excusing myself momentarily, I visited the bridge where the captain was. I took out a small card with the picture of my sailboat and showed it to the captain. Smiling, he gestured for me to take the wheel and steer the ferry. I saw no sign of any instruments, no depth sounder, no compass, no Global Positioning System, no radar, or, for that matter, anything else. I did see many empty holes in what had once been the instrument panel and imagined these must have been removed years before when they ceased to work. I could only imagine the skills required to reach the ferry dock in a blinding rainstorm or foggy conditions. The captain was scruffy but a kind-looking man, with a smile that appeared capable of defusing any situation. After a brief time, I thanked the captain and motioned to him that I needed to return to the stern deck.

I discovered the women and the young girls were all laughing and giggling. Helen whispered to me that the young girls were Kurdish and lived in the city of Diyarbakir, where we were heading. Helen mentioned she had had an opportunity to ask the girls many questions.

Leaving the ferry, we said our good-byes to the young girls and boarded our minibus to begin our trip to the city of Diyarbakir (which means *copper*). Diyarbakir is a bustling city of one million persons, most of them Kurdish. The terrain en route to the city is desolate and poor; the soil color is yellowish and straw-like, with much rocky terrain. Watermelons are a main crop in this part of Turkey.

Looking toward land, I saw a hillside with large white writing. When I asked Anna about this, she informed me that the Turkish Special Forces in this area had inscribed on the mountainside the words "Turkey will never be divided." She went on to explain that, during the 1990s, the PKK had established an underground army for the purpose of creating a separate Kurdish independent state in the eastern area of Turkey. As a result, nearly forty thousand people had died. Until recently, the area had enjoyed a peaceful coexistence within Turkey.

Some Turks feel this problem is the direct result of opening Turkish borders to Kurds escaping the tyranny of Sadam Hussein during the period of ethnic cleansing. Now these same Kurds wish to form their own country. Many Kurds feel they have been neglected by the Turkish government. They lack enough roads, schools, hospitals, and forms of public assistance, support, and equal representation. Kurds have been a historical part of Turkey and will likely always be. The Turkish government is today investing much-needed money and effort into areas of eastern Turkey in an effort to help it regain its rightful place in Turkish society.

There is a massive, impressive wall surrounding the city of Diyarbakir, consisting of two levels. Climbing to the top of the wall, Anna took responsibility for walking us along the top. A young man appeared, and after talking to Anna, accompanied us the remainder of the way. At first, I was suspicious of his intentions and feared he had ulterior motives for accompanying us. I closely watched Anna and took my lead from her reaction to the young man. As she seemed unconcerned by him, I followed Anna's lead and dropped my guard.

He was a handsome lad, well-dressed and groomed, as were most young men in Turkey. Anna learned that he had dropped out of school to make money, although we never learned how he earned his money. We passed a group of young boys burning the insulation off electrical wire to obtain the copper, a valuable commodity to be sold. Although the burning insulation smelled awful, I had to admire their resourcefulness, but I wondered what the end result of this would be upon their health. I had a suspicion that these younger boys were working for the teenager escorting us along the top of the city wall.

Elise, our Australian friend, feared heights but was brave in walking along the narrow way at the top of the wall. We stopped briefly to observe a woman on a rooftop stamping barefoot in a plastic tub, doing her wash. When we signaled that we wished to take her picture, she waved back in approval, smiling and waving to us. As we descended the wall, I suggested we give the young man a tip. Anna attempted, but the young man refused, saying it wasn't enough, adding it was okay, and then leaving.

There continues to be a wealthy Christian community here in the city that's separated from the Muslim district. They speak Aramaic, but also speak Turkish as a secondary language. Christians frequently immigrate to western countries, including the United States, and send money home to support relatives and churches in Turkey. Christians and Muslims live together in harmony here as they have for centuries, each respecting the other. Christian communities and churches are always well maintained and cared for. We visited two very large old Christian monasteries that had few occupants except for several priests, nuns, and caretakers.

When we were back at our hotel, Helen and I discussed her conversation with the young girls on the ferry. Helen described the girls as being similar to any teen-agers found in the United States, but, of course, less privileged. When asked about school, they all said they attended school and hoped to someday go to college if their parents could afford it. One girl wanted to be a teacher, one a doctor, and three weren't sure. Although not certain if they had ever had a McDonalds' hamburger, they all considered this to be gourmet Western food at the top of their wish list.

When asked about boys, they universally answered that their parents didn't permit them to go out with boys. They stressed that girls mostly have girlfriends, and boys have their own friends. This is something I observed throughout Turkey. Even in communities near the marina, I frequently saw young girls holding hands when sitting or walking together. Boys and young men could also be seen arm in arm, walking or sitting together. I've assumed that courting in Islamic culture is considered a serious step that follows strict social and behavioral guidelines.

CHAPTER 4

▼

LIFE NEAR THE IRANIAN BORDER

We visited the Mardin Monastery founded by Samuel (the first monk). It is still active, and the centuries-old building has been restored. Living here are two priests, thirteen nuns, and twenty-five boarding students attending local public schools. Boarding students provide an additional source of income, which is provided by the state for many nonsectarian institutions. Christian monasteries are well maintained and appear to have continuing large maintenance projects currently underway. Although these structures at one time housed hundreds of persons, today they are occupied by very few, with a skeleton staff to maintain them. They charged for tours and solicited additional donations at the end of the tours. We gladly made a small donation, but we couldn't help noticing that we had never been asked for an entry fee or donation at any Muslim mosque or holy site.

Before leaving the grounds, we went in search of restrooms. Walking through the beautiful gardens, we came across several men frantically attempting to revive a small injured squirrel. A gardener applied a water hose, attempting to revive it. Excitedly, they picked up the animal and ran toward the building housing the kitchen. I'd never seen a group of men react this way to an injured animal and thought the more of them for it.

We passed through a small, poor village, practicing a religion best described as being between Christianity, Judaism, and Zoroastrianism (Persian). It is considered to be very superstitious. We saw the antique city of Mardin, with its beautiful lace-style mansion houses now converted to boutique hotels.

Nearby, we once again visited a very poor school, where we donated additional supplies through the teacher. In each school we visited, the students always behaved as if they believed we had come there only to visit them. Because the teacher at this school spoke fluent English, I decided to seize the opportunity to speak with him. Waiting for my opportunity, I sprang on the young teacher when the women began talking with the students.

"Is it okay if I ask a few questions? I travel a lot and am always interested in what people think."

"Of course. What do you want to ask me?" the teacher said.

"As an American, I always wonder how people feel about Americans."

"Turkey was very close to America not long ago. Maybe now we're not as close as we were," the teacher responded.

"What's happened that we're not as close as we were?" I asked, while using my hands to express something very narrow.

"It's not that we're not close, just not as close as we were," the teacher seemed intent upon emphasizing. "I think it's Iraq," the teacher said, seeming almost relieved he had gotten these words out.

"Iraq. Why would Iraq come between us?" I asked.

"Iraq is a major cause of America's conflict with the entire world. Until America ends its occupation in Iraq, America will have many enemies." Following a brief silence, he went on to add, "Even your allies are against you." He stated this in an almost apologetic tone.

Although this young teacher lived in an isolated area, he seemed to have a full grasp of political issues.

Continuing, I asked, "What do you think America should do: leave Iraq?"

"America is the strongest country in the world. It can influence Israel and the Palestinians to settle their differences and bring peace to the Mideast."

Each time I asked a question, I'd hoped the teacher would open up and just start talking, but instead he only answered the questions I'd asked. Continuing, I asked, "If America helps create a Palestinian state, will that bring peace to the world?"

"I think it will go a long way to ending many of the world's conflicts. Until this issue is addressed, there can never be peace in the world. A solution to the Palestinian issue may even contribute to ending terrorism."

"Are you married, and do you have children?" I asked the teacher.

"I'm married, but I don't have children yet. Maybe soon, when I can afford to have children," he responded.

"What are the major issues that face your village? Is it politics?" I asked.

"No, not politics. Politics is for the government to worry about. For us, it's having enough money to buy basic essentials."

"Honestly, how do you feel about Americans?" I asked, hoping for an honest response.

"I'm fine with Americans, and I'm pleased my students have the opportunity to meet Americans. I would like to invite you to stay with us the entire day. My students would get a lot from your being here. You are invited to my house for dinner if you would like to stay. My parents will cook dinner and you can taste Kurdish food."

"I wish we could, but we are on a tour and have to drive several more hours this afternoon to get to our hotel tonight."

"Well, then, maybe in the future," he said in a sincere way.

"Yes, I would enjoy that very much. Maybe someday in the future, then," I said to the teacher, hoping that someday perhaps I could return.

The women finished talking to the children and rejoined us. I believed the children's acceptance of us could be interpreted as acceptance by their parents. I'd learned years before that when children are indoctrinated at home to believe certain countries and people are evil their response is often suspicious and reserved. In our case, the children could not have been more friendly and accepting of us. I had found these same responses when I had traveled around the world years before.

Next, we visited the city of Mardin. We walked the centuries-old and unchanged streets. Narrow streets descended down the hillside, lined with small shops making copper and steel teapots, wooden chairs, Turkish carpets, and all manner of other goods by hand. It appeared to be an area of cottage industries for the wider area. Narrow streets broadened into larger ones with stands of fruits and vegetables outside the shops. Narrow side alleyways with covered stone archways offered protection from the sun. Shopkeepers frequently sat outside their shops prepared to sell goods, but more often to discourse with other shopkeepers. Examining dried fruit in front of a shop, we proceeded to purchase a bag. As we walked the streets, I reached into the bag and put one into my mouth. The dried fruit was hard; it couldn't be eaten. Anna explained that I had purchased the type of dried fruit used to make jam. Because we couldn't eat it, we convinced Anna to offer it to a young boy to be taken home to his mother. He was surprised and delighted at our offer and began running excitedly down the street toward his home. With Anna's help, we carefully purchased more fruit and enjoyed eating it as we walked along the streets.

As we were having lunch in an outside garden café, four well-dressed Turkish women entered and sat near us. Anna, after listening to the women speak, informed us that these were the wives of important judges or politicians. Moments later, the women turned to us and, speaking in perfect English, asked where we were from. After I responded that I lived in Bodrum, she wanted to know how much I had paid for our home, explaining that she wanted to buy a summer home there. I knew that such questions were common and not considered impolite in Turkey. Nevertheless, I replied that you could buy a home at any price depending on what you were looking for. Although I did not directly answer her question, she seemed satisfied with my reply.

That evening, during dinner at the hotel, we observed a Kurdish wedding poolside. We received several invitations to join the wedding, first by the band, then by the family of the bride, and finally by the groom himself. We learned later that women can invite themselves to a Kurdish wedding; only men require an invitation. Twice this happened to us in different hotels; both times we received invitations to attend the weddings. Turkish dancing went on all night; we enjoyed the music and enthusiasm of the guests.

Helen learned the steps by watching and soon found herself part of the evening's festivities. Men danced with men, making up an inner circle, and the women danced with women, creating an outer circle. The men were energetic and moved with harmonious rhythm. The man leading their line held a red cloth and waved it in the air, as they continued to dance to the music and throbbing sound of a drum. The circle took on the appearance of an eclectic mix of dance steps perfected through the years.

Earlier in the day, we had seen another Kurdish wedding taking place in a village along the roadside. I asked Anna to stop, but she refused, explaining that we had to get to the hotel before dark. Reunited with our American archeologist friends at the hotel during dinner, we learned they had stopped at the wedding. They had received an invitation on the spot to join the wedding party, eat, drink, and dance all evening. We reminded Anna we had asked her to stop.

During daylight hours, we frequently offered rides to the elderly and women with children. One morning, we offered a ride to a woman with four children on their way to school. Each of the children was dressed immaculately, the older two boys wearing suit jackets and ties. We learned through Anna that although the government paid for the children to be boarded, this mother preferred to have her children remain at home. Because of this, she was solely responsible for getting her children to school each day. We learned that to reduce the cost, mothers frequently shared the cost of a cab to transport their children between school and home.

Passing a group of young men, Helen and Elise requested of Anna that we stop and offer them a ride. Anna, being an astute guide, put her foot down, saying that to offer a ride to anyone other than the elderly or someone with children was simply not done here. Deferring to Anna's advice, we relied upon her experience in these matters.

We learned from our driver that many trucks carried additional secondary fuel tanks for the purpose of bringing black market fuel from Iran or Syria to be sold in Turkey. We were informed that this fuel could only be purchased by local people and was not available to outsiders for fear of the scheme being discovered. To make his point, our driver stopped at a station and attempted to convince the station owner to sell us fuel from Iran at reduced cost. The attendant insisted they didn't do such things and couldn't recommend anywhere else for us to go. We did see evidence of police and army convoys stopping trucks to inspect them.

To our delight, each night we met the soccer team and our American archeologist friends all heading in the same direction. After the first few days, we grew accustomed to seeing one another and would talk for hours. Whenever possible, the soccer team invited us to see the playoffs. One evening we were planning to leave in the morning and were forced to decline, to the disappointment of Helen and Elise, who fancied the young men. Afterward, each time we passed a soccer stadium, I heard the same sighs of disappointment and listened to the women talk about the athletes.

Unlike western Turkey, here we found isolated instances of children begging, something we were not used to in Turkey. Although Helen and the other women wanted to give the children pencils and paper, Anna frowned upon this practice. She strongly felt it promoted begging and ultimately worked against their social structure. Secretly, I agreed. I've seen situations around the world where parents intentionally prevented their children from going to school so they could beg from well-meaning foreigners.

A problem developed between Glenda and our guide. Anna felt strongly that we should avoid handouts in any form to small children, and, on more than one occasion, this led to conflict between Glenda and Anna. Glenda, on the other hand, felt the children would benefit from a few crayons and coloring books, and since they hadn't asked for anything, it was more than appropriate to make small gifts to the children. At one point, Glenda put her foot down and insisted upon giving the children the crayons and coloring books and chose instead to ignore Anna's advice.

Glenda had a gift for being capable of talking to everyone without the benefit of language. She always found a method of making herself understood, even sometimes using a combination of hand signals, gestures, and a few words of Turkish. Children especially liked Glenda and always approached her when they wanted to know something about our small group. Glenda had never had children or been married. She always showed great interest in and doted upon any child that approached us.

Elise was an attractive woman in her early to mid-forties. She had a wonderful sense of humor and could always entertain us and make light of any situation. Men especially seemed drawn to Elise, and in spite of the fact, she never flirted—they pursued her.

Many times during dinner, we discussed the world's most serious issues and attempted as best we could to solve each one of them. One popular topic was how to avoid war, replacing it instead with peace throughout the world. Both Australian women possessed a keen sensitivity to the basic needs of people and wanted to have an opportunity to change the world by doing just one good deed. Each time this topic arose, we inevitably got drawn into discussing the United States and the world bully we've become since the Republicans took control of congress and the presidency. We spent many wonderful evenings, each sharing our ideas, from the leftist government in Venezuela to the Palestinian issues in the Middle East.

I was often amazed that the four of us—Glenda, Elise, Helen, and myself—although from different countries, seemed to share common views on most issues. I began to look forward to each evening as another opportunity to share our ideas about those things most important to each of us. We didn't just talk about our children, our cars, and sailboats, but about life itself. We all began to let our guards down and share, not only things we felt strongly about, but those things we weren't sure about and needed help to understand.

Driving from town to our hotel, we passed many military roadside stops. On one occasion, we were approached by an officer who pulled open our door.

"Where are you going?" the officer asked.

"I don't know." Looking at the others in the van, I asked, "Where are we going?"

They responded, "We don't know."

The officer smiled and asked our guide where we were going. Satisfied we couldn't be a threat to anyone but ourselves, he bid us a good day and closed the van door. More and more, we began seeing military roadblocks reinforced with personnel carriers, tanks, and serious-looking military hardware. It was clear to us they intended to prevent the intrusion of illegal people, including terrorists, crossing the Iraqi and Syrian borders.

Returning to the town of Diyarbakir, we broke tradition by offering a young man named Ali a ride. I'm certain the fact that he was good-looking had little to do with the women wanting to offer him a ride, and this included Anna. We learned that Ali was a lieutenant in the Turkish Army assigned to UN Forces. He spoke fluent English and traveled extensively throughout the world, including several visits to the United States. Ali offered his services in guiding us to a local shop with the camera supplies we required. I asked Ali many questions.

"Ali, are you Kurdish?"

"Yes," he responded. "I'm a Turkish Kurd, and I was born in eastern Turkey."

"Can I ask a few questions?" I said, hoping for a positive response from Ali.

"Sure," Ali responded.

"Well, it's about the PKK, the terrorists."

"What about them?" Ali responded; his face wore a somewhat quizzical look.

"Are the PKK terrorists from Turkey or Iraq?" I asked, hoping not to offend his sensitivities.

"Both, mostly from Iran, I think. But I'm sure they recruit some ranks from eastern Turkey. Most Kurds from eastern Turkey have lived in and been part of Turkey since the Ottoman Empire and consider themselves to be Turkish. Some feel they have been abandoned by the Turkish government and turned to the PKK hoping to establish a homeland in eastern Turkey. But these are a small minority," Ali said.

I was aware that recently, Metro POLL, an independent center known for carrying out strategic and social studies, had conducted a study in eastern Turkey, where the majority of Kurds live. The results of the study had shown that 95 percent of the respondents indicated they would remain living in Turkey even if a Kurdish state was formed. Most Kurds living in the fourteen largest cities in eastern Turkey indicated they considered themselves to be Turkish, and only 1 percent said they would cross the border to join a Kurdish state in Iraq.

"Ali, how do Turkish people generally treat the Kurds?" I asked.

"Now, that's a question," Ali said, raising his voice. "There's a lot of prejudice against us. We're blamed for things we have nothing to do with. If something disappears, then everyone blames a Kurd for it. When crime increases in Istanbul, then it's blamed on the Kurds. I never get used to it. Do you know, when I was a child, my father wanted to give me a common Kurdish name. He was told he could go to prison for selecting a Kurdish name for his son. That's why I joined the military, to get away from all that," Ali said despairingly.

"Did the military change all that?" I asked.

"Yes! I became a Turkish soldier. Nobody asked if I was a Kurd because I became an officer," Ali said proudly.

Before I could ask another question, he turned his attention back to the women.

Within an hour, we were in the city and dropping Ali off at his hotel. Stepping out of the vehicle, he turned to ask the women if he could come to the hotel later and perhaps have a drink with them.

Elise said, "Call us, and we'll see."

The following day, we were off again. Coming closer to the Iranian border, we observed that the terrain had become more and more desolate and desertlike. We encountered a Turkish military unit inspecting a tractor trailer after they had arrested several scruffy-looking men who were now on the roadside in handcuffs.

After we picked up an elderly man needing a ride, he explained to us that these men were Iranians attempting to cross the border illegally. When we asked what would happen to them, he explained that they would be transported back to the border and passed to the Iranian authorities. When I asked what would happen to the driver who transported the illegal aliens across the border, he informed us he would most likely be held for a few hours, chastised, and sent on his way. I silently wondered if, in fact, he would be incarcerated and fined to ensure there wouldn't be a repeat offense.

Scattered along the roadside were small mud homes, and behind the homes were large tobacco fields with crops ready for harvest. Turkey is the sixth-largest tobacco producer worldwide; Camel cigarettes are a major buyer of Turkish tobacco. Seventeen thousand tons of opium is legally grown in Turkey for medicinal purposes. These crops are closely regulated by the Turkish government.

As we traveled through the mountainous Kurdish area, Anna instructed our driver to stop and offer two young girls a ride home from school. One girl began to climb into the van, but the other said she wasn't supposed to get into any vehicle, and began saying something to her friend who was already inside the van. Both girls became frightened and walked off quickly. I was impressed with their presence of mind and ability to resist adults. Apparently, their mother had lectured them about accepting rides from strangers along this major truck route coming from Iran.

A short time later, we arrived at the largest lake in Turkey, located in Eastern Anatolia. Lake Van is a spectacular sight, rising 1,646 meters above sea level and measuring a total area of 3,713 square meters. In the background, two mountains rise up into the sky, Major Agri and Minor Agri, measuring 5,165 meters and 3,925 meters high respectively. The lake is so large, even on a clear day it's impossible to see from one end to the other. Because Turks prefer the ocean when they are on holiday, there are few places to vacation on Lake Van. Because most of the beautiful lakes are now public lands, private homes are no longer permitted to be constructed. I suspect that the few cottages and small resorts were built long ago and were allowed to continue operation because they were grandfathered. This is in stark contrast to the United States, where waterfront property can be privately owned at premium cost.

That evening, at the Sahmaran Hotel, we met the soccer team and group of American archeologists, and wondered if we were the only tourists in eastern Turkey. As we returned to our room, we noticed massage tables in the hallway, with athletes getting massages in preparation for the upcoming playoffs, Surprisingly, there was no noise or disturbance the entire evening.

In the hallway I met an athlete who had just finished having a massage.

"Can I buy you a coffee?" I offered.

"Sure, why not? Give me ten minutes to shower, and I'll meet you downstairs," he said.

Venturing downstairs, I waited for the athlete at a table near the pool. At first I didn't recognize him without his sweat pants and T-shirt.

"Hi, my name is Abraham," he said, as he pulled a chair from under the table to sit down.

"I'm Ahmed ... from America," I responded.

"Are you and the women enjoying your trip to eastern Turkey?" he asked, in an effort to be polite.

"We are. It's different from anything we expected, and Helen and I are loving it."

"Helen, the pretty one, she's your wife?"

"Oh, yes. Sorry, I thought you knew that."

"Ah, no. I thought maybe all the women were your wives," he said, laughing.

"I wish. One is hard enough," I said, smiling.

"You guys are brave to travel here; we don't see many tourists in this part of Turkey."

"Do you think it's dangerous?" I asked, already knowing I was as safe here as anywhere.

"Of course, as safe as anywhere in Turkey," he said.

"I'm working on a book about Turkey. Can I ask a few questions?" I asked, hoping to get his permission.

"Why not!" he exclaimed.

"That's good. Thanks!" I said in appreciation. After discussing a few more pleasantries in an effort to make him feel relaxed, I sprung my question on him. "So, how do people in eastern Turkey feel about foreigners?"

"Well, I can tell you how I feel about foreigners. I like it when they buy tickets to see us play," he said, smiling.

"I'm serious."

"Serious, huh? Well, then, let me see. Of course, I'm talking now as someone who's visited the United States three times."

"What kind of reaction did you get from people in the States when they learned you were from Turkey?" I asked.

"Most Americans think we're Middle Eastern, and don't even know where Turkey is on the map. Some people thought we were Arabs and asked me if we ride camels. They were surprised when I told them we have nothing to do with Arabs. I make it clear the only thing we have in common with the Arabs is belly dancing. You like belly dancing?" he asked.

"Yes, it's exotic, especially when a beautiful woman does it," I said.

"I think so, too. The women dance for one another, not only for men," he added. "Anyhow, as I was saying: most Americans have no idea where Turkey is and think we all ride camels, carry long swords, and wear turbans. When I tell them we're a member of NATO, they are usually surprised. They're even more surprised when I tell them the Turks originally came from Asia, and our language is close to Finnish. They always look confused, kind of like, *wow!* Everybody always asks me if my wife wears a burka. I tell them my wife wouldn't wear such a thing. I sort of feel like an ambassador for Turkey when I travel to America. Americans don't seem to travel too much. Why is that?" Abraham asked.

"I suppose America is so big, and there are so many different places to see; people are rediscovering their own backyards. I suppose it's a lot cheaper to do that than to spend a lot of money to travel, especially now with the falling dollar."

"Europeans travel; we see a lot of Europeans in Turkey."

"Yes, I know. But Europe is small, and it's much less expensive for Europeans to visit Turkey than Americans," I offered as an excuse.

"Abraham, if I were to ask you what things in your life you were most proud of, what would they be?"

"Another easy one. I would say being Turkish and being Kurdish … for me, they are the same." He said this without hesitation.

"If you wanted to change one thing, what would it be?"

"Hmmm … that's a little harder to answer. Maybe … maybe something that's come to the surface recently."

"What would that be?" I said, trying to encourage an answer.

"Mercy killing," he said, sounding almost embarrassed to mention such a thing.

"Mercy killing?" I said, waiting for an explanation.

Although I had heard of mercy killing, I had never heard it discussed among Turkish people before. A movie shown about mercy killing at a recent foreign film festival brought this cruelty to light for the first time.

"What about it?" I asked again.

"Two years ago, a Kurdish friend of mine who played football for the same league on another team lost his sister to mercy killing."

"What happened?"

"His family was from eastern Turkey. He paid for his younger sister to attend a university in Istanbul. She was in her fourth year and would soon graduate. She began to dress Western-style like all the girls in school. Each time she returned home, her family grew more and more unhappy about the visible changes in her dress and her modern way of thinking. The final straw with her family was when they believed she had brought them dishonor by living with a boyfriend."

"What happened then?" I asked, now intrigued.

"The men met and decided because of the dishonor she brought the family, they had no choice but mercy killing. They appointed her uncle to carry out the death sentence. On her next return home, she was found strangled in her bed. Her brother confronted the other men in her family and even went to the police. After an investigation, her father was accused and brought to trial by the authorities. When it was all over, the uncle went to prison, and the mother would never again forgive or talk to her husband or see anyone in the family again. And my friend was found drowned; most of us believe he couldn't live with knowing his own father had ordered the mercy killing and drowned himself."

"I'm sorry. I didn't intend to ask something so personal," I said. "Does this happen often?"

"People don't talk about it, but it happens all too often. Eastern Turkey still follows many of the old ways. People still maintain their old beliefs and values that are hard to change." He said this with a sense of gloom.

"We don't have to talk about this any more." It was becoming clear he didn't want to talk any more, and I wanted to give him the chance to stop talking about something that he didn't need to be reminded of.

"Are marriages still arranged in eastern Turkey?" I asked.

"Yes, sometimes, but not in the way they were a hundred years ago. Today, families will agree on marriages when children are young. Families no longer interfere if something is going on between a young man and a woman. Families generally respect those relationships today and will leave the young couple to make their own decisions."

"Going on?" I asked.

"You know how it is. When a young girl falls in love with someone she likes. It's different today. Anyhow, few marriages are arranged any more."

"So, some things have changed, then?"

"Some things have, yes," he confirmed.

"Is female circumcision practiced in eastern Turkey among the Kurds?"

"My family would never do such a thing; I'll tell you that now!" he emphasized.

"Yes, but how about other Kurds?" I asked.

"We're not barbarians! I know of no Kurds who do this thing," he said, intent on dispelling any notion that Kurds would ever consider such a practice. "Afraid you'll have to look toward the Middle East for such practices."

"One more question?" I asked.

"Sure," he said, seemingly relaxed with all my questions.

"Well, then. In the village you live in, do you know of people who belong to the PKK?"

"To be perfectly honest, I don't. There are so few of them nobody knows who or where they are. I'm sure there are a few living in Turkey, but I wouldn't know anything about them."

"Truthfully?" I asked, wondering if he'd been truly honest.

"I'm telling you the truth. I doubt I've ever met one, and I sure don't know any or of anyone else that does," he said emphatically.

The way he answered my question I had no reason to doubt his sincerity. I made a point of thanking him for answering my questions so openly.

Saying it was late and he needed to wake for an early morning practice, Abraham excused himself. We shook hands and exchanged e-mail addresses for the purpose of keeping in touch.

Before I knew it, the next day was upon us. We climbed to the top of a hill which had once been part of the Orations' Kingdom. Although only the foundations and several layers of stone block had survived since their construction in 1200 BC, we had a sense of what life had been like here. The castle housed around 150 persons, mostly guards and slaves in service of the royal family. Peasants lived in the valley below. These were a warlike people whose rule was eventually ended by the Persians. I developed an interest in the latrine—the royal toilet was a flat granite stone with a hole in the center and plumbing to transport waste to a septic system. It was advanced even by modern sanitary standards.

As we descended from the ridge, we were approached by a very attractive young Kurdish woman. She attempted to ask us questions, which we didn't understand. Anna, coming to our rescue, talked with the young woman as we continued walking. I noticed that the woman appeared persistent. When I asked Anna what this was all about, she informed me that the woman was very interested in where we were from and where we were going over the next several days. Alarmed, I said, "You didn't tell her, did you?"

Anna responded, "I avoided her questions; she got nothing from me."

"Seriously, Anna, what do you think she was after?" I was very suspicious.

"It's impossible to say. She could have been spying for someone or just a curious young woman," Anna said.

I dropped pursuing the issue further. It was clear we were in good hands with Anna.

The following day, we returned to an area of Lake Van. Boarding a small boat measuring approximately ten feet wide and sixty feet long, we traveled to Akdamar Island to see the ancient church and monastery, which dated back to 915 AD. Our boat was constructed from boilerplate, which was now rusting, and had a capacity for twenty persons and no life jackets.

Unfortunately, the island was closed to the public due to a major restoration project underway and was not scheduled to reopen until the coming fall. We had been told the buildings appeared well preserved and contained beautiful frescoes and mosaics of the period. The structures were large, and many satellite buildings spread out along the island, which had once housed up to 250 persons. Previously, the patriarch of the Armenian Church had lived there until it was abandoned during the formation of the republic. Today, it's estimated that 70,200 Armenians live in Turkey.

Traveling through the city of Van, we observed a modern, upscale city with a population of approximately 500,000 people. High on a hill overlooking the city was the Tushpa castle, built during the eighth century and restored again during the Ottoman period. Instead of climbing to another castle, Helen and I decided to walk the grounds, appreciating the beautiful gardens and local shops.

As we were having tea, we once again encountered our American group of archeologists—this was now an almost daily occurrence. We talked and shared ideas about everything from politics to our experiences traveling around the world. They universally expressed their hope that American politics would take a turn for the better after the upcoming election. Although this is a conversation we normally avoided with others, we added our own personal comments.

Unlike most tourists, these people had spent extended periods in this part of the world, including the Middle East, so I wanted to discuss what they had learned. Opening the subject of how people in this part of the world really felt about foreigners, and especially Americans, I got a wealth of information. At the end of the morning, there was general consensus that adults were less concerned about politics and more concerned about raising and supporting their families, and providing their children with an education and good healthcare. Children, on the other hand, wanted only to emulate Western children, the way they believed them to be from watching television.

In some ways, Muslims and Islamic culture have gone through many of the same stages as Christianity, even if at a slower pace, through the centuries. Those archeologists who had previously worked in Iraq and Iran expressed similar views. Turning to the subject of how extremists are recruited among young people, I heard interesting explanations. One explanation having common support was that young people become frustrated at having no opportunities for themselves. Militant extremist organizations have successfully learned to exploit this frustration to their advantage.

One archeologist talked about how a seventeen-year-old youth had been employed on an archeological dig, giving the archeologist an opportunity to come to know the young man. He described the youth as hardworking; because his father was dead, he helped to support his mother and younger brothers and sisters.

Because of a lack of funding, the dig had been suspended for almost one year. When the project regained funding and the archeologist returned, he discovered that the young man had become a suicide bomber, killing himself and others in a marketplace. Having taken an interest in the youth and gotten to know him, the archeologist described his shock at what had happened. He described the young man as intelligent, sensitive, and even outgoing—always polite, interested in and thinking of others. I could tell from his description of the youth there was an overshadowing sense of guilt over what had happened.

From others, I began to hear of a sense of hopelessness and despair among young people. They felt abandoned by society and were recruited by the thousands by extremists who promised them a better life. One archaeologist made the point that everyone seemed in agreement with: Until the West understands this phenomenon of turning children and young men and women into killers, the violence will never cease. Speaking over the others, another archeologist made the point that these kids only needed to be provided with other choices—then they couldn't be recruited for violence.

His final words to me were: "It's all about addressing their hopelessness and providing something to believe in."

For the remainder of the afternoon I thought a lot about what he had said.

If a group of academics who traveled and sometimes worked here came to understand what motivated kids to become terrorists, why wasn't our government listening? I thought to myself. Where were all our highly paid people at our nation's top think tanks who were supposed to be advising and helping to guide American policy in the administration? Who was wrong here: the group of archeologists and academics or our nation's top advisors?

Once again, I had persuaded Anna to bring us to a restaurant where local people ate. Stopping for lunch, I ordered a bottle of Coke. Although I was given a bottle that looked and tasted like Coke, it was clear to me it was something else because of the missing trademark symbol. When asked, Anna referred to it as *Islamic Coke*, emphasizing that she wouldn't buy it because it contributed to Islamic fundamentalism. Thirsty, I consumed the remaining Coke before agreeing with her; only then did I put down the bottle of Islamic Coke.

Having the opportunity to talk to Anna privately, I shared the fact that freedom of religion was a guaranteed constitutional right and was a fundamental part of our way of life in America. Anna believed that there were Islamic forces in Turkey that would influence it toward becoming a nonsecular government. She strongly believed that if the nonsecularists took control of the parliament, the guaranteed separation between religion and the Turkish government would be threatened by the potential creation of an Islamic state.

CHAPTER 5

▼

KURDISH AREAS

The next morning we left for Muradiye Waterfall and the swinging bridge. The bridge was frightfully narrow and measured some one hundred meters in length above a narrow gorge, and the river was fed by a beautiful waterfall to the side of us.

Although the bridge appeared of sound construction and materials, it did swing when we walked across it. Elise, our brave friend from Australia, tackled her fear of heights by bravely walking across the bridge hand in hand with Helen. I've always admired women who deal with their fears by not allowing them to get in the way of enjoying life. I've found British and Australian women are especially strong-willed in overcoming and dealing with fear.

Once across, we did what all Turkish people do: enjoyed another cup of tea.

Our now-familiar encounter of the group of American archeologists was no different on this day. We became so familiar with one another that passing their bus on the road brought cheers from both groups.

We were now seeing an increasing number of military vehicles and roadblocks, established for the purpose of securing the Turkish borders with Iran and Iraq. Although sometimes we were ushered past roadblocks, this time we were stopped. We saw machine gun emplacements behind sand bags, armored personnel carriers with machine guns pointed toward traffic, and tanks lining the road. The soldiers were young, always courteous and polite, and made every effort to speak English to us. Although on occasion we were required to produce passports, more often they accepted a passenger manifest from our guide.

Because we were identifiably tourists, we weren't subject to the same degree of inspection that more routine traffic was. Truck drivers were required to provide all paperwork and personal identification; often their trucks were meticulously inspected both inside and below for illegal transport of goods, weapons, or people. We were impressed with Turkish military professionalism and thoroughness. Our friends Uri and Tolga were correct—we were safe here.

We saw many trucks piled to overflowing with white bags containing grain. Along the roadside, there were many people waiting for rides to go to work or return home. A short distance beyond the military roadblock, a man carrying his bag of tools waited for a ride. We offered him a ride and learned he had several young children and was returning home from days of working in the city. We offered him school supplies for his children but were informed he had everything his children required. He was a soft-spoken man and clearly looked much older than he was—this explained why Anna had allowed us to offer him a ride. We attributed his elderly appearance to years of hard work in a harsh environment.

Because this area was poor, it became easier to find schools in need of supplies. Each time we stopped in a town, we supplemented our school supplies in preparation for the next village. Arriving in the village of Gorecek, we stopped at a small school, clearly a poor one. As usual, Anna entered first to talk with the teacher, and only after receiving an invitation did we enter. This school had two teachers, both young women.

Although this was the first day of class, the rooms were being prepared to be painted by the teachers and students. Apparently all repair and maintenance of the two-room schoolhouse was done by parents, teachers, and children. The teacher gratefully accepted our donation of supplies, making it clear to us she would inform the supervisor of the school district.

Although I was hoping to ask the teacher the same questions I'd asked at the last school we visited, it proved impossible. Each time I attempted to ask a question, someone interrupted us, asking the teacher's advice or direction.

All of the children were dressed in attractive school uniforms, girls in light blue skirts and white blouses. As we typically saw elsewhere, the boys were dressed in suit jackets and ties. The teacher explained to her students what country each of us was from. When she mentioned America it brought looks of bewilderment. I asked the teacher if her students would like to ask us any questions and said that we would try to answer. As she spoke in Turkish to her students, we heard a flurry of questions.

Turning toward us, the teacher said, "They want to know what video games you play at home in America and Australia."

"You'll have to tell your students we're too old to play video games and wouldn't even know their names, I'm afraid."

As the teacher repeated our words in Turkish to her students, we heard their disappointment in unison. We fielded many more questions relating to music and the latest Hollywood movies.

When we were leaving, the children and teacher followed us outside into the schoolyard to wave good-bye. As I looked back toward the children, I hoped they would remember us and think of Americans as their friends in a world that was quickly becoming more and more isolated due to the haves and have-nots. I silently wondered what their perceptions of Americans and Australians were and whether we had influenced them. Leaving the village, driving along the highway, we saw a new natural gas pipeline under construction, coming from Iran. Turkey can supply only 10 percent of its own oil needs and depends upon outside suppliers. Today, the cost of gasoline in Turkey is expensive, even by European standards.

Not far from the school, we were once again stopped at a military roadblock. Our driver attempted to pass the roadblock, signaling to the officer in charge. We were waved back into line and remained there until cleared for passage. We saw army barracks on both sides of the road with heavy gun emplacements positioned everywhere. Helicopters were nearby and appeared ready to take off.

I'd read many stories of Turkish soldiers over the years and heard a few personal ones told by American soldiers who had had experience with them. The Turkish army had gained the reputation that they should be taken seriously. I'd read accounts that claimed that when they were running out of bullets, they resorted to knives, similar to the British Gurkhas—but they were never known for giving up.

My favorite story was of Ataturk, the founding father of the Republic of Turkey. Although an enemy of the British, he personally approached a British checkpoint, where he was recognized and stopped. He informed the British commander that he and his men needed to pass the checkpoint, and for that matter, the British were on Turkish soil and needed to leave immediately. The British took one look at Ataturk's men and laughed, saying, "Those men aren't equipped to do anything."

"Nonsense!" Ataturk said. "If you don't move or let us through, we will attack you and move you ourselves, but we must pass now. Make your decision."

The commanding officer was so impressed by Ataturk that he instructed his men to allow Ataturk and his few soldiers to pass. There are many stories of Ataturk passing British lines and being given free passage because of their respect for him as an officer and soldier.

En route to our next stop, we stopped along the road for a cup of Turkish tea. Walking through a narrow passageway, we entered a large square surrounded by old decaying buildings with iron gates. I was told this place had once been a commercial marketplace located along an ancient major caravan route. It was a drab-looking courtyard surrounded on all sides by a square building. In the past, the ground floor had contained commercial shops, the second floor had been reserved for the storage of items, and the third and upper floors had been apartments for the shopkeepers. The large courtyard within the buildings had places to wash, a small running stream, and beautiful trees. It was obvious this place was very old and had likely remained unchanged through the centuries. Small wooden tables with very low seats were scattered throughout the square, while young boys rushed about transporting trays of tea. With the exception of Helen, Elise, Glenda, and Anna, only men came here. Anna explained that Kurdish women went to a separate place to socialize and drink tea while their husbands came here. A young, severely deformed boy ran from table to table, asking for shoes to shine. When he came to our table, we gave him our shoes; off he went into the crowd. Within twenty minutes he returned, carrying our brightly polished shoes. Each of us gave him an extra tip; his smile was our reward.

A group of men sat talking at a table next to us. One man leaned toward me, and asked in English, "Where are you from?"

"The United States," I replied.

"Awwww, we don't see Americans here. We don't see any tourists here—they are afraid to come. How come you came here?" the man asked, in a heavy Turkish accent.

"I live in Turkey. I guess I just wanted to see the country I live in," I answered, unsure what to say.

"That's good!" the man exclaimed. "Most people think it's not safe here—that's why they don't come anymore." There was a sad look upon his drawn face.

"Is it safe here for me?" I asked the man.

"Yes," the man said, stopping only to take a deep breath. "Anybody bothers you here, they have to answer to my village, and I'm in charge of the village. That's the way it used to be all over Turkey."

"Which one's your wife?" he asked, looking toward the three women.

"The tall, thin one," I responded without turning.

"How many children you have?" he asked.

Becoming used to hearing this same question again and again, I responded, "We have seven children."

"That's what I have, seven children." As he thought for a moment, his expression gave way to a sudden look as if he had just remembered something. "Don't go up into those mountains," he said, while pointing toward the hills far away. "Stay on the main roads where the army is," he instructed me.

"We plan to stay on the main roads. What's up in the hills?" I asked, hoping to learn something interesting.

"No telling, no telling, but don't go up there." These were his final instructions.

Anna gestured to me that it was time to move on. As I stood to excuse myself, my new friend stood, bent toward me, and kissed me on both cheeks.

Continuing on our journey, we saw Mount Ararat. It's a majestic sight; passing beneath its peak is an unforgettable experience. Mount Ararat is 5,137 meters high and the highest mountain in Turkey. The south and west sides of Mount Ararat are covered in a permanent glacier. Some people continue to believe that the village of Noah and Noah's ark are located on Mount Ararat. The search for this ark and the lost town of Naxuan continues today. Wonderful folklore of this region passes from generation to generation through public displays, reenactments, and word of mouth in many small local villages.

We stayed overnight in the city of Kars. There's a remarkably well-preserved castle on a high cliff towering above the city, giving it a Transylvania-like appearance. That evening, there was a severe thunderstorm that went on for hours. The city lights went out. In the background, illuminated only by lightning, I could see the castle, a sight I will never forget.

At dinner later that evening, we all agreed that the city of Kars was different from all others. It is dismal in appearance, with old barracks-type buildings left long ago by the Russians who were driven out by the Turks. Russian stone architecture can be found decaying throughout the city. Although some has been preserved, much has been lost and is beyond restoration. Few outsiders come here, resulting in little or no outside investment. Without the infusion of money, I see no future for the city of Kars.

I had an interesting discussion with our guide, Anna. When queried about a secular versus nonsecular government, she offered fascinating comments. She reiterated that Turkey has a secular constitution and that it couldn't be changed without revising the constitution or dissolving the republic. She said she would leave her beloved Turkey if it were to become a nonsecular state. She stated that people elected fundamentalist officials because the liberal and progressive officials in the past were fraught with corruption. She said with the election of more fundamentalist leaders, corruption had decreased in government. It was her hope that the secular parties could put forward new leaders who were not corrupt and who would help return the balance of power to a guaranteed secular society in Turkey.

Touring the ancient Armenian capital of Ani during the early morning hours allowed us to see these ruins at the perfect time of day. Strangely, we were the only people there. It is an immensely large area and is located on the border with Armenia. Observation towers are visible on both sides and give evidence to the recent tension between both countries during this century. Until recently, coming here had required army or police escort at all times, but this is no longer necessary. At one time, this city competed with Antioch as one of the great cities of the region because of its importance in trading and business. Unfortunately, the Armenian capital never recovered to its previous glory following the Mongol attacks, and today it sits decaying.

The large Armenian cathedral, constructed of immense heavy stone blocks, was the largest of its period. Standing at one end of the church and looking toward the altar, I began to appreciate the immense scale of the church. We visited one small church on a hillside whose colorful and beautiful frescoes adorned both the inside and outside of the building. The history of the saints was still clearly detailed but in risk of damage through natural erosion and water damage to the building. Antiquities are so numerous in Turkey that preservation and restoration of all is impossible because of the magnitude and cost.

While there, I attempted to engage Anna in a discussion about the Armenian issue of genocide. Although she always answered all of my questions, she became noticeably quiet when it came to this topic. Her silence caused me to realize how passionately Turkish people felt about this issue. I would never know her true feelings on the Armenian question.

We drove many hours through the Yanliz Gam Mountains, whose appearance is similar to the Swiss Alps. The steep mountainside and gorges below were thick with pine tree stands rising high up the cliffs. The hillside was covered with Swiss-chalet-type homes. This type of construction was different from anything we'd seen in Turkey. It was obvious the builders of these homes had used whichever local materials were available for construction. Exterior wooden porches, now mostly used only during the warmer months, encircled the homes. We were told winters were so cold and severe in this region, travel was restricted by the harsh, wintry conditions. Stopping at a roadside chalet-style restaurant, we enjoyed wonderful pan-fried trout.

Our final destination was a visit to Sumela Monastery, constructed upon a steep cliff of the Black Mountains. The original name was Our Lady of the Black Rock; it had been founded by two monks from Athens, Greece. As it was impossible to drive to the top, we climbed the remaining distance along narrow trails before finally reaching the beautiful clifftop monastery. Occasionally we passed a single line of Turkish people forming a procession climbing upward. Once inside the monastery walls, we saw many separate buildings of a village-like style, each for different purposes. Some housed monks, others kitchens, visitors' rooms, chapels, study halls, and libraries.

The church was established in 412 AD by two brothers, both monks. The monastery was in continuous use until the republic was founded following World War I. During this time, all Greeks (Greek descent) were required to leave Turkey and return to Greece. The same was required of Turks (Turkish descent) living in Greece. Because there were no clear borders prior to these times, the descendants of Greeks and Turks were frequently intermarried. Returning Turks and Greeks often had to re-adapt and learn to speak an unfamiliar language as though returning to a foreign land. On more than one occasion, people have expressed to me that forcing Greeks and Turks to relocate from their homeland of many centuries to a foreign country was a sad and cruel point in the history of both countries.

On our way to spending our last night at the city of Trabzon, we passed through the cities of Artvin and Rize. In Trabzon, I pointed out the small picturesque boutique hotels to Anna. Laughing, she informed me that these were brothels, where Russian women were employed.

In the more mountainous regions, we saw children and adults with light skin, blue eyes, and red or blond hair—a testament to the influence of Georgia and the extent to which the Ottoman Empire had once ruled.

After an unprecedented eleven-day trip through eastern Turkey, we were now preparing for the flight from Trabzon back to Istanbul. We stayed one evening in Istanbul, returning to our home in Bodrum the next day. Our exploration of eastern Turkey had surpassed our expectations. We had seen a different side of Turkey, one we will always appreciate and remember fondly. Like all the Turks, the people of eastern Turkey were hospitable and friendly to us.

When I returned to Bodrum I was besieged by neighbors and friends wanting to know if I had enjoyed eastern Turkey and what it was like. My response was always met with surprise. I began to appreciate that telling many Turks that I had gone to and enjoyed eastern Turkey was little different from telling Americans I was going to Gaza on holiday. I realized I'd learned my first lesson: things aren't always as they are presented to us. I was now prepared for my next adventure and even bigger challenge—the Middle East.

CHAPTER 6

▼

THE EASTERN
MEDITERRANEAN YACHT
RALLY

Helen and I now prepared for our next exciting adventure. I decided it might be easier to travel to countries such as Syria and Lebanon in a sailboat with an international rally. In this way, I could enjoy less travel restriction and have the freedom to go places I otherwise would not be allowed to go.

It occurs to me that the reason sailors are accepted at face value throughout the world is that in traveling the world one can become part of it. Sailors become international citizens and spokesmen. Traveling opens our minds and spirits to different people and their cultures.

I've known many yachtsman and yachtswomen who have resisted the temptation to become political when traveling throughout the world. As sailors, many have learned to avoid the political pitfalls and keep the way open for those sailors who will follow. The people I met throughout our circumnavigation were interested in the same things people everywhere are: feeding their children, educating them, enjoying good health and a future to look forward to.

The Eastern Mediterranean Rally has drawn more than eighty boats each year for the past seventeen years, which have visited Turkey, North Cyprus, Syria, Lebanon, Israel, and Egypt, before returning to Israel where the rally officially ends. The yachtsmen are Muslim, Christian, Jewish, Buddhist, and other denominations. The common denominator of love for the sea has helped all of these yachtsmen to forget their differences. Instead, they create a common bond of friendship for life. By visiting foreign lands, each yacht becomes an example for international peace, cooperation, and brotherhood.

Our first challenge was to notify my marine insurance company of our intention to sail to Middle Eastern countries and to expand my policy to include these areas. Their response was not surprising. The insurer wanted to make me aware that a war might break out at any moment and that the U.S. State Department had issued travel warnings for those countries I intended to visit. My broker informed me that the insurer was taking a dim view of my travel plans from an insurance perspective. I wrote back that their policies always excluded acts of war or armed conflict, so they needn't be concerned, and if they didn't want to cover me, then the broker should find another insurer. A few days later, I received a hefty bill for my expanded coverage, which I paid.

In preparing for the rally, I gave consideration to taking on crew, due to the many overnight passages. After reviewing a long list of potential crew people, I narrowed our list to just a few. Helen was permanent first mate aboard *Tahlequah*, and she had a good friend, a young British woman with whom she spent many hours studying. Each morning, Jackie came to our home for two hours to study Turkish. Helen was an experienced sailor, and Jackie and her partner had a boat and home next to ours. Jackie's partner, Ian, would be away for three months, volunteering his skills in Cambodia, and because of this, he encouraged her to crew with us. Jackie agreed, and we now had the necessary crew.

Having known Jackie personally for a few years, I decided to practice my intended questions on her before trying them out on others. "So, Jackie, how do the British feel about Americans?" I asked.

"They think Americans are know-it-alls and never shut up," Jackie shot back at me.

"Oh!" was all I could think of to say in response to Jackie's directness.

"What do Americans think of the British?" Jackie asked.

"I don't know about other Americans, but I hate those white socks and sandals they wear to the beach. It looks dumb!" I said, wanting to get in my own digs. Jackie just laughed and then went about what she was doing.

Although in previous years there had been more rally participants, this year the total number of yachts was reduced to sixty-two, fewer than in previous years. I attributed this to the politically unstable situation in the countries we would be visiting. As an American, I would be reluctant to sail to Syria and Lebanon on my own. Sailing with a large international rally which had been in existence for seventeen years has its benefits, one being security.

Traveling to far-off places and talking to everyday people gives me a unique opportunity to get a snapshot of what and who the people are in these places. I've always believed that people's opinions are often a more powerful driving force than reality. Politicians have learned to respond to surveys of public opinion in securing votes, which may in the end have nothing to do with fact or, for that matter, the best interests of the country. I was interested and driven to understand the people in places that had been presented to me over the years as anti-Western and even hostile to Americans.

I asked myself one question: *If the people of one country can come to know the people of another country, won't empathy follow?* Popular views of the people are frequently seized upon by those wanting to make a career of politics. An educated public can be more powerful than the potentially misguided judgment of one man leading a country. It would soon be my turn to come to meet and know more people from other countries.

The rally came from Istanbul to Turgutreis on May 3, 2007. After the usual cocktail parties and dinners, we set sail for a seventy-nautical-mile cruise down the Turkish coast, stopping at Marti Marina. The Turkish coast guard sent a new cutter with crew of twenty-five to accompany us through Turkish waters. We noticed a Doberman pinscher running around deck and assumed he was the ship's mascot. After tying off to the dock, two crewmen emerged and began erecting a portable doghouse (painted in military colors) at the side of the gangplank. Each time we approached the boat, the dog insisted upon playing with us—the first sign we were not dealing with a guard dog.

The coast guard was always invited to our parties and other social occasions. At each formal dinner, the Eastern Mediterranean Rally members, specifically Hassan, our leader, arranged to personally recognize and thank the coast guard by presenting the captain of the vessel with a beautiful rally commemorative plaque. It was during one such occasion that the captain made a speech saying the Turkish coast guard, if needed, would come to our aid, no matter where we were. His statement made me wonder if the Turkish coast guard was intending to transit and remain in international waters during our multinational Eastern Mediterranean Rally. Although logistically impractical, his words were intended to reassure us that Turkey gave great importance to our rally.

Turkish coastal waters are especially clear and clean. Because there are more than fifty thousand commercial sailboats during the height of tourist season, and many more private sailboats and mega yachts, the Turkish coast guard has the responsibility of enforcing environmental water standards. Coast guard helicopters fly above marinas looking for would-be scoffers who ignore environmental regulations. This can be the result of grey water and waste discharge or non-biodegradable soap being used for washing the boat. Frequently, marinas are held accountable for these infractions, and heavy fines are levied against the marinas and boats when they are identified. A benefit we've realized when looking out toward the open sea is that it's possible on a clear day to see the sea bottom within a few hundred yards of shore.

The Turkish coast guard is a well-funded, manned, and equipped fleet maintained to the highest standards. It possesses the latest hardware, including ships, helicopters, and aircraft. They take flying the ensign seriously. We once observed the coast guard approaching a sailboat without ensign and crew aboard. Believing the crew to be at a nearby beach club, they entered, requesting that the crew return immediately to their vessel. In Turkey, flying a national ensign is done with a sense of pride. Even a torn ensign is considered a violation of etiquette, and the owner is responsible for replacing it immediately. On one occasion, the coast guard circled *Tahlequah*, inspecting our ensign. Fortunately, Helen had sewn a frayed edge only the day before.

We were disheartened when, while we were staying at one marina, it became obvious some boats were guilty of pumping directly overboard. Because most yachtsman and marinas work hard at obeying the laws and leaving a clean wake, the practice of dumping directly overboard is the exception rather than the rule. Those who do break these rules are sometimes discouraged by a limited number of pump-out stations or the necessity to sail several miles offshore, contributing to the overall difficulty of obeying the rules. I was pleased to see that our home-port marina occasionally inspected the waters for contamination. On one recent sailing excursion, when we climbed the hill overlooking the anchorage, we came upon a group of soldiers observing the yachts below. Although we did not know their precise purpose, we guessed they were there in search of illegal discharge coming from the anchored yachts.

Night after night, we were treated to cocktail parties and formal dinners requiring the men to wear jackets and ties, and the women nice dresses. We learned to enjoy Turkish dancing, where men dance with men as well as women. Turkish dancing can be compared to Greek dancing and is an expression and outpouring of the soul to the wonderful beat of lively Turkish music.

During this time, we met the crew of one of three Turkish boats participating in the rally. Although our language skills were limited, we always managed to communicate through a combination of a few English words, Turkish words, and sign language. They had a small boat with six crew aboard, and we wondered how that many people could manage to get along so well. Barely squeezing into their cockpit, we joined the crew one evening for sundowners. Their good will and enthusiasm were exceeded only by their inspiring attitude toward others, both in the rally and the countries we visited.

We worked our way down the Turkish coast, stopping at Port Gocek, Kekova Roads, Finike, Kemer, and Alanya. As we sailed down the Turkish coast, stopping at marinas along the way, we were joined at each stop by additional yachts participating in the rally. Although we spent three to four days at each location, this time was divided among all-day tours, social events, cocktails, and dinner parties. While in Finike, we signed on for an all-day tour visiting the cliff caves of Myra, a Lycian city, and Akifalar. There had been a misunderstanding, and a German tour guide had been provided instead of the agreed-upon English-speaking guide. At the end of the day, a few of us may have even learned a few new German words in spite of the fact that we learned nothing about the sites we visited. Everyone took this major faux pas in good humor.

We found the rally to be well organized, with all details carefully thought out. We paid a basic US$300 per crew person. All marinas were free of charge, including water and electricity. Even dinners and cocktail parties, including liquor, were paid for by the marinas or municipalities. In places where there was only a commercial fishing harbor, all local boats were asked to leave during the time of our visit. In each case, the fishermen displayed no sign of displeasure and even collected money to provide a fireworks display for our entertainment. In addition to these things, we received rally polo shirts, briefcases, and beautiful plaques at the end, commemorating our participation in the rally.

Because there were sixty-two boats, it was necessary to divide these into separate groups, based upon cruising speed. Fortunately, we were in group six, the fastest group. This meant we were always the last to leave and the first to arrive and secure dock space before the others. Reporting our position every four hours became a routine rally procedure. Sailing at night surrounded by sixty-two boats to keep an eye on can be a bit troublesome at times and was something we weren't used to. We used our new AIS radar to locate ships in the area, thus reducing the risk of collision with the big boys. During the rally, there were two known collisions between rally yachts and a few near hits. One problem we encountered repeatedly was boats using incorrect navigational lights. Again and again, the same boats used anchor lights at sea instead of steaming lights to indicate they were under auxiliary power.

Rallies have aroused controversy among yachtsmen since they first began. Because yachtsmen tend to be independent people, who sometimes think of themselves as the last explorers, rallies are sometimes discredited. Many yachtsmen think of rallies as glorified tours that take away the freedoms enjoyed by life aboard. I look at rallies differently, and see that, like most things in life, there's an upside and a downside. Sailors join for different purposes: some for safety in numbers, some for easier entry into places infrequently visited, some for a speedy voyage, and many simply for the lasting friendships made.

CHAPTER 7

▼

NORTH CYPRUS

Our next destination was North Cyprus. Greek mythology says that the goddess Aphrodite arose from the sea here.

In 1974, the island of Cyprus experienced a coup, which forced out the president and ultimately resulted in the Greeks taking control of two-thirds of the island and Turkey taking control of the remaining area. The conflict resulted in the Turks relocating to the Turkish Republic of Northern Cyprus and the Greeks likewise relocating to southern Cyprus. A United Nations peacekeeping force now separates both factions, and Nicosia, the capital from the tenth century, is still a city divided by the "Green Line."

Leaving the port of Alanya, we sailed ninety-six nautical miles overnight, to Girne, North Cyprus. The first evening of our arrival, there was a cocktail party in our honor at the beautiful crusaders' castle located on the waterfront in Girne. The castle was a Venetian fortress and was surrounded by buildings from the same period. The entire castle had been closed to the general public and reserved for our cocktail party. The castle itself was a remarkable one and was in the best condition we'd seen. There, we were given a presentation by a representative of the president of North Cyprus; the president himself had been called out of town at the last minute and was unable to attend.

We took a day-long tour to monasteries, crusader castles, and many other local sites. The tour guide asked if we wished to see the "ghost town," explaining that this was the dead zone between North and South Cyprus, adding that he would arrange lunch at a nearby hotel if we agreed. Without exception, we all agreed; we wanted to visit the ghost town. We drove past what appeared to be miles of barbed-wire fencing dividing the dead zone from the small town we were in. It wasn't until we sat on the hotel veranda overlooking the beautiful shoreline that the realization of what we were looking at fully struck us. Imagine seeing Miami Beach with its hundreds of luxury hotels, streets, and businesses totally abandoned and cut off from the outside world.

It was a surreal scene—it could have come from the movie set of *War of the Worlds*. Only then did we come to fully understand the tragedy of what had happened here in Cyprus. An entire major city had been abandoned for fear the Turkish army would come to inhabit it. We were told by the guide that when the Turkish army did arrive and discovered it to be empty, they encircled it with barbed wire, leaving it as it stands today. Many of the luxury high-rise hotels beside the ocean are now on the verge of collapse, with their sides crumbling, exposing the interior of the buildings. Towering structures and expensive apartment buildings all suffer the same fate. It was obvious to us this had been a major vacation and tourist area in the early 1970s and would have been today if not for the conflict in Cyprus. Standing there on the veranda looking toward the city, few of us could speak; instead, only the clicking of our cameras broke the silence.

Hearing of these things on television does not do justice to the price paid for conflict. Throughout the Mediterranean, there have been repeated examples of wars for thousands of years. Each ancient ruin and castle has been attacked and sacked many times. In each case, these attacks have left only death and destruction in their wakes. Although it's easy to accept thousand-year-old wars impersonally, it hits home to see a modern city left in ruins.

We found North Cyprus to be much like Turkey but with an English flavor because of early English colonial rule. Many Northern Cypriots speak English, which explains why there are many British expatriates living there. The language is Turkish, and the economy is based upon the Turkish lira. We find the same friendliness and hospitality in North Cyprus as we've become used to in Turkey. I cornered several English-speaking Turkish Cypriots to learn their feelings toward Greek Southern Cyprus. In each case, I sensed no hostility toward the Greeks. Surprisingly, they expressed a desire for the reunification of Northern and Southern Cyprus.

Many ex-patriots have purchased property in North Cyprus on which to settle down and retire. I've speculated on how risky purchasing property in North Cyprus is, because the European Union doesn't recognize the legality of land holdings there. Although Turkey has remained steadfast in its support of Northern Cyprus, I have to wonder what challenges will be made to the legality of these Northern Cyprus land holdings when Turkey becomes a full member of the European Economic Community.

I couldn't help but think that Greek Cyprus becoming a member of the European Community might damage the opportunity for reunification of the island. Having previously circumnavigated the world, I've seen evidence again and again that the will of the people doesn't always reflect the will of their political systems. The news media, too, sometimes lend themselves to this complicity.

We were told prior to coming to Cyprus to be prepared for the Pirate Party, one of the main gala events of the rally. I purchased a pair of Turkish baggy black village pants, black shirt, and coffer and brandished a menacing-looking cutlass. Adorned by two wenches at my side, I was off to the Pirate Party. A bus transported a total of 220 "pirates" to the castle located on the waterfront. Although authentic, the town of Girne appears like a movie set from the early 1500s, complete with taverns, buildings, and cobblestone streets restored to the style of the times. It's remarkable to me that the town could have remained as it was for so long.

Led by hobbling fifers and drummers, we began our parade along the waterfront, singing old sailing chanteys. "What do you say to a drunken sailor?" became our anthem. Every restaurant and pub emptied into the streets to see the likes of us.

I heard one little girl tell her mother in English, "Mommy, I'm scared of the pirates!" The English pirate in front of me pulled behind him a wench bound in chains. I must say, after seeing this group: We could put any Hollywood wardrobe to shame.

At the end of town, we were once again put on buses and driven to a hotel for dinner and party. There, we were taken to a large banquet hall to celebrate our arrival in North Cyprus. Following routine introductions and formalities, we were informed we could expect something which had never been done before in North Cyprus. A group of young Greek Cypriot dancers had crossed the border that morning to attend our party and dance with their counterparts, a Turkish North Cypriot group. A man explained to us in English that this would be the first time Greek and Turkish dancers had performed together publicly in Northern Cyprus since the division. Because Greeks and Turks had lived together for so many centuries, their dances were very similar, and we could only separate them by costume.

As the young Greeks and Turks began to dance together, a hush swept over the crowd. Suddenly we all began to clap and keep cadence with the ever-increasing rhythm of the music. The music and dancing were infectious, and each of us began to clap our hands, stomp our feet, and make every noise and gesture possible to become part of the performance. We could tell that even the dancers were enjoying our reaction. When it was over, there wasn't a dry eye amongst us.

Each of us knew what we had witnessed—music and dance had brought two peoples together and had succeeded where war had failed. Unrehearsed, one person stood to clap, then a second, until all were standing on their feet, cheering the dancers, as I doubt they've ever been cheered before. Only after the dancers left the room did things return to normal. As sailors, we've traveled to many countries and far-away places. We've become used to conflict throughout the world and have sometimes become hardened and desensitized to it. What we witnessed that evening will remain with each of us always.

CHAPTER 8

▼

SYRIA

One practice we were introduced to was the Rally Flag Ceremony before formal dinners. There were sixty-two boats, containing crew of 222 people, representing seventeen nations. At each flag ceremony there were flags representing each of the seventeen nations in the rally. Each of the flag bearers stepped forward to say a few brief words to honor his or her host country. On one evening, an overzealous flag bearer went on so long that a rally director had to take the microphone away from him.

I came to appreciate the two people responsible overall for the rally; these were Hassan of the yacht *Ibis II* and David of the yacht *Mashona*. Hassan was Turkish and had been managing the Eastern Mediterranean Rally since its inception in 1990. He was a master of public relations and gifted at solving any problem with good humor. Hassan had the God-given talent of making everyone feel good about doing something they didn't want to do. David was Hassan's right-hand man during the rally and excelled at achieving results, even when it came to taking the bull by the horns. Like the rest of us sailors, David recognized the value of meeting people in far-off places and making friends with people sometimes demonized by our news media at home.

Hassan valued his role in being an ambassador of goodwill and did everything possible to keep our minds and hearts open. I believe that Hassan wanted all of us to return to our home countries as spokesmen for the wonderful places and people we had met during the rally. We all recognized both David's and Hassan's talents and knew we would return home safely with their guidance.

It was finally time to leave North Cyprus for another overnight sail to Mersin and then Iskenderun, eastern Turkey. After a few days in Mersin and Iskenderun, we left for an eighty-five–nautical-mile overnight trip to Lattakia, Syria. Before we left Turkey, the captain of a Norwegian yacht berthed alongside ours asked me if I would like to borrow a Canadian or Norwegian for the trip to Syria and Lebanon.

His face became sterner, and looking at me seriously, he said, "Have you thought about having a smaller flag? That's a pretty big one."

Smiling, I said, "Haven't you heard? Size matters."

Deep down, I understood his fears. His fears were no different than my own when I had circumnavigated the world several years before. As I had traveled through Malaysia and Indonesia, the largest Muslim populations in the world, I had at first feared people's reactions to my American flag flying off the stern. Only by traveling to these countries did I experience firsthand their hospitality and friendliness toward everyone, including Americans. Wherever I traveled, people always made the distinction between people and their governments.

Knowing we were headed for one of America's adversaries, Syria, I was now more excited than ever. Syria was historically known as Mesopotamia and has many archeological and historical sites. This would be another major opportunity to make up my own mind about Syria and the Syrian people. I was armed with questions; my goal was to find Syrians with whom I could communicate.

Although we were requested to remain outside Syrian waters until reaching exact coordinates, a few boats prematurely ventured inside Syrian territorial waters. Because of this, the fleet was requested to immediately stop and head 180 degrees offshore. Once the Syrian navy was satisfied with our cooperation, we were given permission to proceed to the Lattakia Syrian Yacht Club. Because the rally directors had made every effort to stress the importance of cooperating with the navy, I could only assume some hadn't understood due to language issues. Outside the harbor, we were circled by local fishing boats, with people waving and hollering to us. To my delight, the Syrian fishermen waved and cheered upon seeing my large American flag flying off the stern and continued this until we entered the marina.

Entering the yacht club marina, I was surprised to see an American flag flying prominently in front of the yacht club office with the flags of all the nations participating lining the sides of the marina. I assumed this to be their way of making all the yachtsmen feel welcome to Syria. I was pleased to see that yachtsmen in Syria, like all other places, continued to rise above politics.

The view from the marina surprised me; the city appeared to be a modern one with newly constructed condos and stores. Syrian customs officials were there to greet us and expedite our arrival into the country. That evening, the yacht club gave a formal dinner in our honor. As the temperature continued rising as we ever so slowly moved south, I disliked having to wear a jacket and tie and would have preferred shorts and a polo shirt; unfortunately, we had no say in this matter. The Syrian army was assigned the responsibility of our security and set up checkpoints around the marina and even on the dock itself. Each time I passed a checkpoint, everyone smiled and waved. I was later told by an English-speaking Syrian officer that a general had been assigned to oversee our safety.

The yacht club took responsibility for arranging a two-day tour to Damascus and Palmyra. We visited the old city of Damascus, reputed to be the world's oldest inhabited city at almost four thousand years old. Much of this part of the city remains Christian, and one can find small ancient chapels along the many narrow, winding streets. Some are several levels below ground level because of the changing elevation of the streets throughout the centuries. As I entered one small chapel, my eyes had to adjust to the lack of daylight. By the light of only a few prayer candles, I saw elderly women sitting and kneeling in prayer. Unaware of my presence, they went about their daily adorations. Walking through Christian basilicas, mosques, narrow streets, and souks of the old city, one could get lost for days absorbed in the sights and smells of this exotic city from the past. The many shops and bazaars of this city are not for tourists but for Syrians coming to bargain for the many things for sale here. Because we were on a tour, we spent far too little time here and regretted having to leave so soon.

We visited the Damascus National Museum, a remarkable museum, containing wonderful examples of exquisite mosaics, Roman and Greek statues, sarcophagi, and an underground tomb. The highlight of the museum was a completely relocated synagogue with original frescoes from 200 A.D. Because the synagogue had been buried for centuries beneath sand in the desert, it had escaped decay and destruction. The entire synagogue had been rebuilt, including the outside walls and surrounding courtyard. Sitting inside on the stone seats was for me a very moving experience. Looking at the frescoes depicting scenes from the Old Testament, I was moved to think how many people had come here for guidance and inspiration. Reading the museum flyer in English, I took note of the emphasis—this was considered one of the most important exhibits in the museum. Sitting here in the darkened corner of the synagogue, I was saddened to think that

Jews were prohibited from entering Syria and would never see this wonderful exhibit.

Although we paid only US$35 per person for the tour (all inclusive), surprisingly, we were treated to a five-star hotel, the Edam Cham, which was located on the outskirts of Damascus. A similar hotel in the United States would have cost above $350 per night.

After a gourmet dinner and good night's rest, we arose the next morning to travel to the city of Palmyra, also known as the Queen of the Desert. It was a remarkable sight to approach these ruins (partially reconstructed) midafternoon, as the sun began to cast its shadow upon the beautiful limestone columns, roads, buildings, and statues. The light-colored limestone melted into the yellowish sands, and with heat rising from the desert floor created a visual panorama, like something seen through a kaleidoscope. Unlike most world heritage sites, there are no modern cities or dwellings in the background to distract from this incredible site. The site is a massive one and seems to go on forever. Seeing the city from different vantage points contributes to the understanding of how impressive it once was. All that was missing was people.

We were entertained with postcard and water-bottle vendors attempting to make sales any way possible. Once we passed a vendor, he would jump on a bicycle or motorcycle and speed down the road to cut us off and begin again. This enterprising effort went on during the entire afternoon, and eventually, the vendors escorted us back to our coach.

Everywhere we traveled we saw pictures and posters of the president of Syria. Every storefront, home, and bulletin board displayed his picture. We were informed that the president had just been reelected and that the people were overwhelmingly supportive of him. Seeing all these pictures did make me wonder whether this was genuine or coerced. I asked the question tenderly, and our guide informed us that their president was the son of the previous president and had done much to liberalize the country since replacing his father. He was loved by the people, our guide informed us.

In the countryside we saw many Goliathlike statues of the previous ruler and father of today's president of Syria. Knowing this man was an iron-fisted dictator, I had difficulty believing that anyone truly worshiped him. I couldn't help but recall, in my own professional career, sitting in the senior staff room, hearing others postulate how they respected the person in charge, when, in fact, outside this room, he enjoyed little support even among his own senior staff. It was only when this person was replaced by another that the truth emerged, and so this art of deception went on and on.

In real life, people often say and sometimes do what they believe those in charge want to hear and see. I've always believed that surrounding oneself with people whose purpose is to agree with and rubber-stamp another's wishes is a true sign of weakness in any leader, but it is a pitfall for many. Personally, I don't believe this is a shortcoming of only dictatorships and despots but is alive and well within the democratic political process today. I'm reminded of the previous U.S. secretary of state, Colin Powell, who told his president what he believed he needed to know. It can be reasonably assumed that because he did not fully support all administration policies his resignation was accepted by the president. Colin Powell's successor, although a brilliant woman, became a mouthpiece voicing support of all and anything the president displayed inclination to do.

I knew from the Western world's perspective that Bashar Assad, the president of Syria, while recognized for increasing personal liberties, was overall regarded as carrying on the policies of his father. Like his father, he was considered a threat and, at best, a frustration to the West. Syria, for many years, had been accused of interfering with and taking advantage of its neighbor's political instabilities and exploiting these to its advantage to become a leading and influential power in the Middle East, much like Iran.

Everyone I talked to believed that the military was the true force behind the country and that any attempt by the president to give too many freedoms would result in a military coup. They truly believed their new president would continue the reforms he had begun during his first term as president. When I asked about the specific nature of these reforms, I was told by an English-speaking Syrian that, previously, foreign cars couldn't be imported except by politicians. Sending children to school was costly, as was medical care. Borrowing money through a bank was highly regulated. Now Syrians were free to vote to elect their officials who, in turn, elected the president. According to this man, all of these things had been liberalized with the promise of more to come. Without saying so, I couldn't help but wonder how free the people really were to vote for the candidates of their choice.

Privately, I asked a Syrian if he believed, as the world does, that Syria was behind the assassination of Prime Minister Harari, of Lebanon. Without thinking, he responded that he believed the Syrian military might have played a role, but he was convinced the president was not involved. Like all of us, he could only guess at who was involved in this heinous crime, but I was more interested in his response to the question.

When I asked the authorities if I was free to walk the Syrian streets near the yacht club without escort, I was informed I could go anywhere and talk to anyone I wished. Taking advantage of this opportunity, I left the marina and walked throughout the town. I never traveled anywhere without wearing my Australian bush hat. The hat had become my signature over the years and, on more than one occasion I believed it had been disarming and often the first topic of conversation.

Although most Syrians on the streets didn't speak English, it wasn't impossible to find a few shopkeepers who did speak limited English. I enjoyed a cup of tea with one shopkeeper who was as interested in me as I was in him. Once we were both comfortable with one another, I brought up the subject of his impressions of the United States. He didn't hold back, and I got more than I asked for. He began by making the same point that everyone else makes, including Europeans. That is to say his problem with the United States was with our American president and not Americans as a whole.

In the middle of his dissertation about American politics, he stopped to ask, "Do you think Hillary will win your next election?"

"There's a chance of it," I answered.

"I hope so," he said. "Bill Clinton was a good president. People listened to him. He listened to the Palestinians."

"He did at that; he was a good president," I responded.

"Do you think America will attack Iran?" he asked.

"I don't know, but I hope not. I think a year from now things will be different, with a return to diplomacy to settle our differences. Maybe even a solution to the whole Palestinian issue," I added.

A big smile appeared on the shopkeeper's face. "I hope so," the man said, as he continued to drink his tea.

"We hear Americans don't like Syrians; how come?" the shopkeeper asked.

I thought for a minute before answering his question. "Well ... most Americans believe that Syria is providing arms to Iraq, and that's killing American soldiers. Do you think that's true?" I asked.

Without hesitation, the shopkeeper shot back, "America arms insurgents in Iraq, who cross the Iranian border to kill innocent people. So why shouldn't Iran arm insurgents to protect themselves? Did you know that?"

"I did read about that in the *London Times* and heard it again from Jimmy Carter," I responded.

"So, what do you expect Iran to do?" The shopkeeper seemed confident he was making his point.

"I'm not sure. I recognize that Syria and Iran are neighbors of Iraq, and the reality is they are both a part of the problem and a part of the solution." The shopkeeper now seemed intent on grasping my every word. "Maybe with a new president, we will sit down and talk," I said.

Just then, I saw a man come from behind a curtain at the back of the shop, carrying a broom. As he began sweeping the floor, I asked, "Does he work for you?"

"Yes," the shopkeeper replied. "He's Iranian," he added. "Would you like to talk to him, too? I can translate."

"That's great," I said, barely able to contain my pleasure at having an opportunity to talk to an Iranian.

The two men talked together for a short time before the shopkeeper turned toward me, saying, "What do you want to ask him?"

"Well, let me see." I was going to get right to the point. "How do Iranians feel about 9/11?"

"Nine/eleven?" the shopkeeper asked in a way that made it clear he didn't understand my question.

"I mean the World Trade Center bombing."

Turning toward his employee, the shopkeeper began talking, and although I couldn't understand, they spoke to one another for almost two minutes.

"He says a lot. He says after 9/11, the students from the university led riots in the streets. There were big demonstrations."

"Why?" I asked.

The two men began talking again. The sweeper was now becoming excited, and I could tell that whatever he was saying, he had strong feelings about it.

"He says that everyone was upset and angry that this bombing was an insult to Islam. They wanted the people who did this caught and punished."

"I don't think Americans had this impression," I said, adding, "Ask him what's changed between Iran and America."

Again, the shopkeeper began talking with the sweeper before turning toward me once again. "He says that Iran wanted to show its friendship to America after the bombing, but Bush threatened and insulted Iran many times, and we became angry. We felt America didn't want our friendship."

As another customer entered the shop, the sweeper suddenly returned to the rear, where he once again began sweeping. Not certain if the shopkeeper didn't want to continue talking in front of a customer, I pardoned myself, thanked them both, and said I needed to return to the yacht club. Inviting me back, he shook my hand, and I returned to the waterfront.

On another occasion, I resumed walking the local streets in search of others who spoke English, but didn't have the good fortune to find anyone.

One evening, after returning to the yacht club from our two-day tour, we were taken by bus to an outdoor restaurant, complete with a large waterfall, massive trees with lights, and live entertainment and music. The dining halls would have suited a sultan.

Suddenly, we began to hear what at first sounded like gunshots. Looking skyward, we saw the night sky illuminated by fireworks. The fireworks appeared to come from every direction, and car horns went on all night. A waiter explained that the fireworks were in celebration of the president of Syria being reelected.

On the return bus trip to the marina, I saw beautiful estate-like homes lining the main highway. Asking to whom these homes belonged, I was told they were owned by politicians. The people of Syria were warm and welcoming, but in spite of this, I couldn't help but wonder how many freedoms they actually enjoyed.

CHAPTER 9

▼

LEBANON

Leaving Syria, we began another overnight 105-nautical-mile trip to Jounieh, Lebanon. I knew only two things about Lebanon. The people were the descendents of Phoenicians, and Lebanon is considered the most Westernized country in the Middle East. Jounieh is today known as the playground for the wealthy of Beirut, which is only a short distance away. We were excited and looked forward to visiting Lebanon.

We were provided coordinates by the Lebanese navy, which we strictly followed. Just after entering their territorial waters, we were met by a Lebanese naval cutter, which escorted us into the Jounieh Marina and yacht club.

We were surprised to arrive at a five-star yacht club in this part of the world. On walking toward the office, we passed many exotic sports cars and mega-yachts. Bikini-clad women walked throughout the complex, and those who were dressed appeared to have come straight from Paris. It was clear to me that these people were the privileged and in no way could they represent a true cross section of the population of Lebanon. The complex contained an Olympic-size swimming pool, restaurants and shops, and several tennis courts for members.

The first thing I noticed there was the intense security at the front gate and on the grounds. We were informed that the president came every morning to swim, as did some cabinet ministers. A car entering the yacht club was electronically scanned for explosives before it could enter the property, and only members were permitted to enter. Special armed forces patroled the large property, keeping an eye on safety and security. I did notice that when the president swam in the pool there seemed to be additional security. There was a certain tenseness in the air as though everyone feared something terrible might happen at any moment.

The first thing we discovered in Lebanon was that nearly everyone spoke Arabic, French, and English. For this reason, we were able to communicate everywhere and at every level. The president of the country is Christian, and the prime minister is Muslim. The Christians today are a minority and represent less than half the population. They are outnumbered by the Muslim population. Since the devastating civil war that destroyed Beirut, the Christians and Muslims have learned to live and work together. Unfortunately, most agree that their differences continue to be exploited by their neighbors for political gain.

A Lebanese (Christian) woman named Mary stopped to talk with us at the yacht club. She had come to pick up her children after tennis lessons. Our conversation during the next hour helped form my impressions of Lebanon.

Her first words were, "You're with the rally," after which she added, "You are very brave people, and we respect you for coming here to be with us, as no one comes now."

There were tears in her eyes as she talked about the threat of violence in Lebanon, and how after thirty years of this, she had never become used to it. She talked about how the Christian sections of Lebanon had been mostly supportive of Israel until they had been bombed during the last Israeli-Lebanese conflict. We personally saw the many destroyed bridges and roads now under reconstruction in the Christian areas outside Beirut. These bombings resulted in much widespread confusion and loss of support in Lebanon for Israel, according to the woman we talked to. Mary was concerned that because of this conflict, their fragile democracy, one of the few in the Middle East, was now threatened by new forces from within.

Mary put her arm lovingly around her teenage daughter, saying, "I want my children to know peace."

A short time later, Helen returned from the ladies' room. As she exited with another woman, they reached forward to shake one another's hands. Instead, both women spontaneously hugged and began to cry. When I asked Helen later who the woman was, she described the conversation which had occurred in the ladies' room. The woman, upon seeing Helen enter the ladies' room, had asked where she was from. Helen had explained that she was here with the rally and looked forward to seeing Lebanon.

"You are brave to come here now. It's dangerous even for us," the woman said. "We're so tired of war here. That's all there is, and we're on the brink of civil war. It will never end," the woman described tearfully.

"So that's what we talked about. That's why we hugged and cried leaving the showers," Helen said.

I knew that many Lebanese blamed the United States for not using its influence to stop the Israel-Lebanese conflict. Behind every conversation, I knew this was always looming in the background. One honest person asked me if America didn't understand how divisive Israel's invasion had been and how it had pushed Lebanon to the brink of destroying their fragile democracy. I made no attempt to explain American policy in the Middle East.

Within the first two days of being in Lebanon, we were beginning to hear of bombings in the city of Beirut. It was suggested that we not enter the city at night, as it was no longer considered safe. We did visit the rebuilt city of Beirut in daylight hours.

Just as we approached the city, we entered the street where Rafik Harari, the beloved prime minister, had been assassinated by a car bomb three years before. The road had just this day been opened, and our vehicle was stopped, while young men handed out white long-stemmed roses to the women. Posters and billboards of Rafik Harari could be seen throughout Lebanon as a reminder of how important a figure he was to the people and their liberation from Syria. It was Harari's money that helped rebuild downtown Beirut after the civil war in Lebanon. He is now buried in front of the mosque he built in the center of the city.

To enter the rebuilt city of Beirut, it's necessary to pass through several layers of military security. Our backpacks, packages, and pocketbooks were searched as we passed through scanners at the city gate. All the buildings have been rebuilt with limestone and marble, and this small section of the city has truly returned to being the "Paris of the Middle East." We could still see bullet holes in the front wall of the parliament building. We were told that parliament had not met for some months due to the fear of bombings. Because of the recent threat of unrest and bombings, we saw military and tanks everywhere, even outside Beirut.

I was surprised to discover that the downtown area, although completely restored, was also totally empty. Tables and chairs outside restaurants, upscale clothing stores, jewelry shops, even a new Starbucks, sat empty. No people, with the exception of us, were on the streets. It was an eerie feeling walking the deserted streets block after block. It felt as if we were on an empty movie set, awaiting the arrival of actors and extras to shoot the next scene. Upscale New York, London, and Paris chains had stores here that mostly remained closed.

We visited the museum of antiquities in Beirut. It was a small, but beautiful, museum that had been restored by private donations following the end of the war. Seeing a film, we learned that during the civil war the building had been used by snipers and had mostly been destroyed. Fortunately, the museum curator had sealed many of the larger antiquities in concrete before placing them in the basement for storage. Had he not had the forethought to do this, all the antiquities in the museum would have been lost forever.

I hoped that by meeting and talking with both Muslim and Christian Lebanese, I could develop an understanding of how the Lebanese saw their future. As an American, I wanted to learn how the average Lebanese on the street viewed the United States. Although Muslims and Christians living in Lebanon have learned peaceful coexistence since their civil war, outside interests continue to exacerbate their political differences, maintaining instability within the country.

The country is today divided into two political groups: those who want a close alliance with Syria and those who do not. Because of the assassination of politicians who are against Syrian involvement in Lebanon, many claim Syria is trying to force Lebanon to depend upon and be controlled by Syria. Most people I talked to believed that Lebanon's future and fate is being defined by outside influences. In spite of this, I continued to get a sense that the Lebanese first wanted internal stability and peace within their own borders, then peace and stability with neighbors outside their borders.

We were all aware that the situation in Lebanon was growing more serious daily and were unsure how this would affect us. A group of terrorists had sought refuge in a Palestinian camp after killing several Lebanese army soldiers. The government surrounded the camp and demanded they surrender, or the army would bomb and enter the camp. Hezbollah demonstrations and bombings were happening now daily.

After much thought and discussion, only a handful of us decided to tour the ancient city of Baalbek and Anjar. Baalbek, located in the fertile Bekaa Valley, is a designated World Heritage Site and an outstanding example of Roman ruins. The Baalbek acropolis is one of the largest in the world. It is commonly referred to as *Heliopsis*, which means "city of the sun." Because of the perceived danger of passing through Hezbollah-controlled areas, some rally participants elected not to go.

In Baalbek, there is a massive temple to the god, Baal, the sun god. It cost the lives of 100,000 slaves to construct this temple, sections of which remain standing today. En route to Baalbek, we passed through Muslim villages with banners in support of Hezbollah. It was common knowledge that Hezbollah had financial support from Iran and provided free schooling, medical clinics, social programs, and other benefits to those living in Hezbollah-controlled areas. In one sense, it's a means of buying the hearts of the people. At each historical site, there were T-shirt vendors selling shirts with the Hezbollah green symbol, a rifle raised in the air. Some of those on our bus purchased these shirts to bring home. Fearing the money from these shirts was supporting a militant political organization, I refrained from buying one.

I had a private conversation with our tour guide. One of the things she mentioned was that, on one tour, she had been required to bring a group of tourists to listen to a leader of Hezbollah, a very charismatic man. She never informed her parents, for fear they would make her quit her job as a tourist guide. I reminded her she was a grown woman. She smiled and explained that because she was still single, she was required to live at home under the care of her parents. Because she was unmarried and living at home, her parents had the right to make her quit her job or any other such decision.

Because our guide was educated and knowledgeable, I asked her why she believed Afghanistan had given refuge to and supported *bin* Laden after the World Trade Center bombing.

"Let me explain," she said. "There is a well-known story in the Middle East. A very wealthy and influential man came home one day to be told his son had been murdered. He hired men to find the murderer of his son but without success. Years later, the wealthy man gave a party and afterward invited his guests to stay. One man, who was his son's murderer, stayed to later become a confidant of the owner of the palace. In time, the murderer felt guilty and could no longer bear the burden of his secret. He went to his host, confessing he was the murderer of his son. The father was angry but knew this man was a guest in his house, and tradition would not allow him to take revenge upon his son's murderer as long as he remained. As a Muslim, he could not throw his invited guest into the street, so he offered the man a small fortune to leave his home immediately. All Muslims understand this concept. You see, because bin Laden had fought against the Russians, he had remained a guest and could not be expelled and turned over to the United States. Can you understand what I said?"

"Maybe ... but on a practical level, I think it's a difficult concept for Westerners to grasp. I mean the story is a beautiful one, but bin Laden was himself a terrorist, who represents a threat to the entire world."

"Yes, but it's our culture," the guide quickly responded.

I wanted her understanding, and she provided it. I thanked her, and we began to talk about our next stop.

I asked a Christian person why Hezbollah had suddenly gained new strength in Lebanon, even among the Christians who traditionally supported both Israel and the United States. Without hesitation, she responded, "For the first time, Hezbollah did something that our government and military couldn't do."

"What's that?" I asked.

"Hezbollah defended Lebanon. If it weren't for them, Israel would have invaded Lebanon with ground forces. Hezbollah prevented them from doing that," the woman said sternly. She added, "That's why Hezbollah has support here."

I heard this same explanation again and again. Like any country, the people of Lebanon were proud, and repelling any invader of their country evoked a sense of patriotism and brought people together. I wondered if Israel truly understood the price they paid for this war.

Sensing an opportunity, I asked our guide "Could you arrange for me to meet with someone in Hezbollah?" adding, "Maybe an insider who could answer my questions?"

"I could lose my job for endangering your life," the woman responded defensively.

"I apologize, then. If not you, is there someone else I could ask?"

"Impossible! You don't know what you're asking." the woman said, sounding more determined than ever that she would play no part in helping me. I would have to look for help elsewhere.

One highlight of Lebanon was visiting the Jeritza Grotto, deep in the earth. Until recently, the grotto had been used as a munitions storage depot by the military. Recognizing its importance as a national treasure, it was converted to a tourist attraction. To view the lower grotto we had to ride a small electric boat through the beautifully illuminated caverns. Stalactites and stalagmites projected from the cavern ceiling and floor and lay shimmering in the artificial light provided for us. Some of these were massive and looked like mushroom-shaped nuclear clouds. As I looked at these, I began to imagine all sorts of creatures, some trapped in motion.

Later, we walked to the upper grotto that paralleled the lower caverns. Here it was possible to walk almost endlessly through the breathtaking caverns. The walkways appeared to be suspended in space high above the Grand Canyon-like areas below us. After walking for more than an hour into the caverns, we stopped at an overlook and gazed into the abyss below. A young New Zealand woman began to sing a beautiful Maori love song. We were all left with tears in our eyes. Later, we visited the ancient Phoenician city of Byblos. Much excavation is happening there, but at that time we saw only foundation ruins.

On the return trip to the yacht club, we passed a sculpture that had been given to Lebanon by an American sculptor to commemorate the end of the civil war and serve as a monument to those who perished in it. It was a tall obelisk-like cement structure that rose twenty meters into the air. There were large randomly placed cavities to make it possible to see what was inside the obelisk. Tons of weapons including a tank, large field artillery pieces, automatic weapons, and all other kinds of articles of war were encapsulated inside the concrete monument. When I saw the monument, it expressed for me a fitting end to the killing tools of war and prevention of their use ever again.

Two days before leaving Lebanon, knowing that this might be my last opportunity to talk to someone belonging to Hezbollah (a Shiite Islamic political and paramilitary organization), I developed a plan. I arranged through the yacht club for a taxi with an English-speaking driver, which is easy to do in Lebanon. After I indicated that I wanted only to see the area between Beirut and the yacht club, we began driving and talking. During our discussions, I learned that the driver was a Christian, had retired from the Lebanese military, and was now a teacher. Like most people in Lebanon, he wanted only peace for his country.

Feeling it was the right moment, I said, "I'm writing a book to explain all points of view in the Middle East, and I wanted to talk to someone from Hezbollah."

"Is that right?" said the driver. "Well, maybe it's your lucky day. If you want to talk to someone, maybe I can help."

"No time like the present! Can you take me now?" I asked the driver.

"Now? You want to go now?" he said, sounding surprised.

"If you have the time."

"You're paying me! You're the boss," the taxi driver said, visibly pleased at his windfall for the day.

Suddenly our taxi crossed the highway, turned, and picked up speed. As we cruised at around eighty kilometers, I could see the Beirut skyline in the distance.

"Are we headed to Beirut?" I asked.

"The outskirts of Beirut," he responded, in a way that suggested he did this every day.

"Do you know this person well?" I asked.

"He's my cousin," he said, as if suggesting that I should have already known this.

"I guess you know your cousin pretty well, then. What can you tell me about your cousin?" I asked.

"He's a Christian, like me."

"Well, then, are you a member of Hezbollah?" I asked.

"No, not me. I want no part of them." Anticipating my next question, he continued, saying, "Some Christians have begun supporting Hezbollah since the recent Israeli-Lebanon War. They defended Lebanon and stopped Israel from invading Lebanon. I think this all started when Israel began bombing Christian areas. They never did that before. Before, many Christians supported Israel."

"I have to turn here," the driver said, excusing himself from continuing our conversation.

A moment later, we were on a side street of small industrial shops and warehouses off the main avenue. Old, barely legible Arabic signs were displayed above the shops, whose names I was unable to read.

"We're here," the taxi driver said, as he rolled to a stop in front of a small shop. "Come with me."

Following him into the shop, I saw automotive parts everywhere; some were cluttering the old, oily wooden floor. Others were stacked one atop the other to the point of falling over. A group of men were sitting at the rear of the shop, talking to one another in Arabic. I observed one man holding a piece of paper, while running around pulling items off shelves and placing them into a hand-held basket. I was amazed that although the place looked to be in disarray, this man appeared to know exactly where everything was and had no difficulty locating each item on his paper.

Approaching the counter, the driver leaned over and kissed the cheeks of the man, then said something to him in Arabic.

"This is my cousin, Memmet," the driver said.

"Hi! I'm Ahmed," I shot back, as I extended my hand to the man.

"What country are you from?"

"America," I responded.

"America? We don't see Americans here," he said, sounding surprised at my answer.

"What religion are you?"

"I was raised Christian," I said, wondering where this was going. Without thinking, I asked, "If I had said Jewish, would it have made a difference?"

"Nah, nobody cares if you're Jewish or any other religion here. But we have something in common; I'm Christian, too," Memmet said with a disarming smile. "My cousin says you're interested in Hezbollah."

"Yes. Did your cousin explain why?" I asked.

"He did. Yes," the man said. "I'm probably not the right person to answer your questions. But what do you want to know?"

"I would like to ask you a few straightforward questions."

"Go ahead," Memmet said, now sounding relaxed.

"Some people think that Hezbollah is behind the political killings in Lebanon and is being driven by Syria," I stated.

"Some in Hezbollah believe Israel is involved in these killings," Memmet replied.

"Yes, but what do you think?" I asked.

"I used to believe that Syria was involved. Now, I'm not so sure."

"Did you join Hezbollah of your own free will?" I asked.

"Yes, of course," he answered, surprised I would ask such a question.

"How do you feel about Americans?"

"Americans. You mean about George Bush," he said in a way that left no doubt he was angry at even the mention of his name. "George Bush tried to blow Lebanon out of existence," he said, his voice now shaking.

"I'm American. How do you feel about me?" I asked, hoping I hadn't pushed the limit.

"Did you vote for him?" Memmet threw this question back at me.

"No! I didn't. I'm a Democrat," I exclaimed.

"Then I have no problem with you," he said, to my relief. "Israel did America's bidding here," he said, leaving no doubt as to what he believed and intent upon convincing me.

"Are there a growing number of Christian Hezbollah supporters, and have you fought for Hezbollah?" I asked.

"There aren't many Christians supporting Hezbollah, but the United States is forcing it upon us, and the numbers are growing. A few of us support them because they do more about defending Lebanon than the government."

"Have you fought for Hezbollah?" I asked for a second time, wondering if he preferred to avoid my question.

"No! I've demonstrated with Hezbollah against Israel, but I've never fought with them. That's something different."

"How's that different?" I asked, hoping for an honest response.

"My older brother and mother wouldn't be pleased. I might even have to leave home," he said clearly, leaving no doubt that this was something he didn't want to have to face in his life.

"Do you talk to your brother about this?"

"We've argued many hours about this. He's the oldest in the family, and he could forbid me if he wanted, but he hasn't. He's sworn us all not to tell our mother."

Thinking for a moment, I recalled how as a young man I had held back from telling my own mother many things I knew we would disagree about.

"I understand," I said, giving evidence of only a slight smile.

"Do you know Hezbollah militants?" I asked.

"Why do you want to know?" he asked.

"I'm writing a book, remember? If I wanted to talk with such a person would it be possible?" I asked.

"I don't know. Even if it were, it would take a few days."

"It wouldn't work then, we leave soon for Israel," I said, disappointed this wasn't going to work out.

With that, I changed the subject. "If you could say one thing to Americans, what would it be?" I asked.

"One thing …" he said, as if he wished he had more time to consider his answer carefully. "I'd say to Americans that Lebanon is your friend. We're the only democracy in this part of the world, and unless you help us, Lebanon won't survive. That's what I'd say!" he said, now sounding exasperated.

I intentionally reduced the level of our discussion by asking, "What are the most important issues for you personally?"

"Making enough money to take care of my parents and my children." His voice was now calmer than it had been a few moments before.

"What do you want for your children more than anything else?"

"I want peace in Lebanon for them," he said, with a hint of reverence.

"Do Christians think of Hezbollah as a terrorist organization?"

"Look, there's nothing clandestine about Hezbollah in Lebanon. It's legal to belong to Hezbollah and legal to support them. They help people; they pay for schooling and medical assistance; and they are a political force here in Lebanon. That's all there is to it."

It is no secret that Hasan Nasrallah, as the head of Hezbollah, formed a close alliance with Iran and Syria and receives close to three hundred million dollars a year from Tehran. He has close ties to the Syrian president. His influence in Lebanon is unquestioned, after he forced Israel to withdraw from Lebanon in 2000 and resisted an Israeli incursion in the last war. His communication skills at providing an image for Hezbollah are paralleled only by his military tactics and methods of successful guerilla warfare.

"And your parents truthfully aren't aware you belong to Hezbollah?" I asked.

"No, and I won't tell them," he said matter-of-factly, for a second time. His words were beginning to leave little doubt in my mind we had moved to the end of what he felt comfortable talking about.

Someone from the back of the room began an exchange of words in Arabic with the shop owner. At first, it was difficult to determine whether they were talking or arguing. As the voices grew louder, there was no doubt that they were arguing. I'd forgotten that everyone in Lebanon spoke English, and the men at the rear of the shop had been listening intently to our discussion.

Turning to look back at me, the shop owner said, "I'm sorry. I have to get back to work."

Thanking the shop owner for talking to me, I followed the taxi driver back to his car. When I asked the driver what they had been arguing about, he told me that one of the men was concerned about his talking to me. When I asked him why, he said that there were other Christians who might be upset if they knew he was a Hezbollah supporter.

Thinking for a minute, I asked the driver, "Why would Christians be upset if they knew he was a Hezbollah supporter?"

"That's a simple one to answer. No one knows who is behind all these political assassinations. Many suspect it's Syria, and everyone knows Syria provides money to Hezbollah and has spies everywhere."

"What do you think matters most to kids in Syria?" I asked the driver.

"Kids are kids. Every kid wants what all kids want."

Which is?" I asked, hoping to get him to talk more.

"What he sees on television."

"And you?" I asked.

"Me, well, I guess I have something in common with my cousin. I want peace in Lebanon, of course. But I want to be successful and live to see my grandchildren have families of their own. I want to see to it they have more than I did growing up." Following a brief silence, he added, "I only drive a cab on weekends; otherwise, I'm a schoolteacher."

As I sat silently in the cab, a picture began to emerge in my mind. For some unknown reason, I began to think of something that had happened many years before, during a business trip to China. It had to do with a personal experience, making me realize we can come from different backgrounds and still respect one another. Traveling to China and working with the same men for many years, I had developed a comfort level with them and we frequently discussed both business and personal things. I was in China during the Tienemman Square violence.

At a late-night dinner, I requested an oath from my close Chinese friends. "If our countries ever go to war, we must promise that none of us here at this table will ever fight one another."

Following a moment of silence, the senior Chinese member of our small group lifted his glass, saying, "I give my word to our oath."

Everyone then raised his glass and said the same. The senior Chinese member at that table was also a high-ranking member of the Chinese Communist Party.

Twenty minutes later, we were back at the yacht club.

"We're here," the driver said, as the automatic door locks sprang open.

I had begun to feel the driver was trustworthy, and thinking quickly, I blurted out, "If I wanted to talk to a Muslim and someone very active in Hezbollah, would that be possible?"

"When do you leave with the rally?"

"In two days we leave for Israel."

"I might know someone, a teacher and friend I work with at the school where I teach."

As the words came from his mouth, he was already unclipping his phone and raising it to dial someone. As he spoke in Arabic, I had no way of knowing what he was saying.

Lowering his phone, he asked, "You want to talk to someone because you're writing a book about the Middle East, and you've written other books?" He asked this, wanting me to confirm what he already knew.

"Yes," I said, without further comment. The driver continued talking in Arabic and in words only he and his friend could now understand.

"Is tonight all right, between 10:30 and 11:00, outside the marina?" the driver asked.

"Yes. I don't want to go anywhere in a car. Ask him if we can meet in the pub across the street from the marina."

As he continued to talk into the phone, the driver began nodding.

After a few seconds, the driver put his phone on the dashboard, turned to me, and said, "Okay, it's all set for 10:30 tonight." A few seconds later, he continued, "Almost forgot. He says you can't use his name in your book. Is that okay?"

"No problem. I can't remember Lebanese names anyhow," I said, attempting to reassure him.

I spent the remainder of the afternoon by the yacht club pool, writing down a list of questions I wanted to ask. Reviewing these, I finally rolled up the paper into a ball and threw it into a garbage bin near the table.

What am I doing? I thought to myself. *I'm not a journalist or news reporter. All I want to do here is have an intelligent conversation so that when I write about Lebanon, I can fairly represent all sides. After all, I'll be talking to an educated man, a teacher. I'll just let our conversation progress naturally and ask him questions that come to mind.*

I now had a plan and looked forward to this evening.

As the time of our meeting grew closer, I was becoming nervous. As I entered the pub, there were young men and women sitting everywhere, listening to the sound of loud, throbbing Arabic music, occasionally interrupted by music with familiar Western lyrics. Sitting at the bar, I ordered a beer. Looking around, I searched the room for whoever I was to meet, a challenge made more difficult because I had no description of who this person was. I knew only that he was a friend of the taxi driver, a teacher, and an active member of Hezbollah. Growing anxious and looking at my watch every few seconds, I developed a nervousness I rarely experienced. The people sitting and standing at the bar could have been people anywhere. Many of them were well dressed and appeared to have stopped for a drink after work. Women were standing in groups together, while men attempted to make eye contact with some of them. Each time I thought someone at the bar might be my contact, it became clear he was there talking to friends or distracted by something else.

As I was lifting my glass to consume the final few ounces of beer, I felt a hand on my shoulder. Surprised anyone could sneak up on me from behind, I turned, to be greeted by a young, thin, friendly looking man, dressed in a suit jacket and tie. He appeared like any young professional stopping off at a pub on his way home from work after a long day at the office.

"You're Ahmed?" the stranger asked, as he continued to rest his hand on my shoulder.

"Yes, I am," I said.

"What kind of name is that for an American?" he asked.

"It's a long story. Anyhow, that's what they call me in Turkey," I said, hoping I wouldn't have to explain the entire story of how I got my name.

"I see. Everyone just calls me Fatiah." The letters smoothly rolled off his lips. "My friend told me all about you. You're writing a book about the Middle East."

"Yes, I am," I responded.

"My friend said good things about you. He said you seemed trustworthy."

"That's good to know. You both work together?" I said, hoping just to sound interested.

"Yes. We both teach at the gymnasium level."

"What do you teach?" I asked, as if this were the next logical question to ask.

"Several subjects, actually. I teach English and biology."

"That explains why your English is so good," I said with a smile.

"Actually, I did my undergraduate and graduate studies in the UK. I lived there for seven years, and, besides, most people in Lebanon speak English. Actually, Lebanese learn French first after Arabic, because it's hard to learn French if you learn English first."

"I never knew that," I responded. Motioning to the barmaid, I gestured for another beer for my new friend.

"So, what is it you want to ask me?" he said.

"Let me begin by explaining I'm attempting to write a book that bridges what as an American I've come to understand on the evening's news and reality on the street." Seeing the look of confusion on his face, I continued trying to explain. "What I'm trying to say is: Many Americans draw conclusions based upon the evening news, which stresses countries' adversarial political differences. Contrary to that, I'm attempting to write a book that allows normal everyday people to understand one another without political filters. Does that make sense?" I asked my new friend, Fatiah.

"Yes, of course. I understand what you're trying to do, but do you think anyone will listen to you or, for that matter, even publish your book?"

"Honestly, I don't know."

"Have you ever published a book before?" he asked.

"I have. It was a book about circumnavigating the world. Actually, I've written four books but only published one."

"Why is that?" Fatiah asked inquisitively

"I couldn't get an agent or publisher to read my books, let alone publish one. Finally, I published one myself using my own funds."

"And?" Fatiah asked.

"Well, it did win a few prizes in literary contests, but in the end, I only sold a few hundred copies."

"So, why do you write then?"

"I don't write to make money, or I wouldn't be doing this. I retired early, and I write because I feel I have something important to say. You see, I've been sailing around the world and going to places most people only read about. It's brought me into contact with people and cultures that have changed my attitudes about the world, and I have a passion for writing, so I write about it. Afraid it's as simple as that."

Taking a few seconds to regain my breath, I continued, "So whatever you share with me probably won't make the front page of *The London Times* or the *Larry King Live* show. The way I look at this, if I can share a balanced picture of the world with two or three hundred people, then we're all moving in the right direction."

Waiting patiently for me to finish, he began to squint in anticipation of his turn to say a few words. "That's a noble cause, but do you think anyone really cares?"

"I can only do my part; the rest is up to the person reading what I have to say. If it speaks to their condition, if it makes average people like us stop and think about their prejudices, then maybe in some small way, we've changed the world."

"So, what is it you want to know?"

"Were you fighting Israel during the Israeli-Lebanon conflict?"

"No. I'm a schoolteacher, but I know many people who were involved in fighting the incursion of the Israeli army into Lebanon."

"Look, instead of my asking questions, why don't you talk about what's important to you?"

"The most important thing to me is solving the Palestinian state issue. Without a peaceful settlement, the violence has already spilled over into Lebanon and is now in danger of spilling over into Syria and Iran."

"Fatiah, do you think Israelis and Palestinians are closer to solving this problem than they were, say, two or more years ago?"

"No! I don't think so. Now that Gaza and the West Bank are politically divided, there's less chance of settlement than ever. The Israelis have what they want—the Palestinians fighting amongst themselves."

I could tell that Fatiah no longer had to be prompted; the passion of his words had become clear. "Look, how can Israel seriously negotiate with the Palestinians about statehood when they continue to build Jewish settlements on Palestinian land? Maybe only 10 percent of Israelis are fanatical, but they are the ones who believe they are God's chosen people and that God gave them Palestinian lands to occupy and build on. The Israeli government has turned their back to Jewish settlements on Palestinian land since the Six-Day War and is continuing to do it even today. Sure, they close a few settlements for the news media, but then the settlers just occupy trailers in the same places, and they are protected by Israel.

"The people of Gaza today are living in Jewish-created camps, surrounded by barbed wire. They can't leave to work, they can't leave to go to school, and they can't even get out for emergency medical care. Even the basic fundamentals have to be approved by Israel—fuel, water, food. Israel is making it more and more difficult for Palestinians. Today, even moderate Palestinians have openly lost faith in a peaceful solution to Palestinian statehood."

"Fatiah, what do you say to those who accuse the Palestinians of terrorism?"

"The Palestinians don't have planes, bombs, and artillery supplied by the United States to engage in a Western-style civilized war. The Palestinians have to throw rocks and engage in any means at their disposal to promote their cause because they have been forgotten by the rest of the world. I will tell you this, friend. Until the Americans insist upon Israel seriously engaging the Palestinians, terrorism throughout the world will worsen, not just for the West, but for the entire Middle East."

"Do you promote violence as a means to solve the Palestinian problem?" I felt compelled to ask Fatiah.

"No! I don't promote violence as a solution, but I won't condemn them for fighting to free themselves from the inhuman barbed-wire prison Israel has put them in. Are you aware that the United Nations has approved close to four hundred resolutions over the years condemning Israel for many of its actions?"

Choosing to ignore his question, I went on to ask, "Your students, do they share your opinions, and are they aware of your feelings?"

"We're careful in school not to voice personal opinions on subjects that even teachers are divided on. We have strict guidelines to avoid divisive subjects. More than half our teachers are Christian and have traditionally supported Israel in the past; although, since the last Israeli conflict, some no longer support Israel."

"Yes, I keep hearing that. But what do you want for Lebanon?"

"What everybody wants. Like Americans say, *I want all this shit to end.*"

"Fair enough, but I have one last question for you. If I were to ask you for a list of the most important things in your life, starting with the most important, what would that list look like?"

"That's an easy one to answer. My wife and children are the most important things in my life. After that, I suppose, Lebanon, after all these years, finally realizing peace. The thing I fear most is another civil war, something the United States and Israel have almost brought us to the brink of."

"It's my turn now; can I ask you a question?" he asked, seizing the opportunity to turn the tables on me. "When I lived in the United Kingdom, I sensed people were made to feel that to question Israel risked making them sound anti-Semitic. Isn't that true in the United States?" he asked, sounding as if he were now conducting some major study and not coming across as attempting to trap me.

"I never thought about it. I suppose I would be reluctant to criticize Israel without considering carefully how it sounded."

"Then you are afraid of coming across as anti-Semitic," he said pointedly.

"I suppose so. I mean, I would be careful not to offend anyone," I added, trying to figure out my own feelings on the matter.

"Now, let me ask you. Is it possible you would be much less prone to criticize Israel than any other country?"

"I want to say, *no*, but I might be. I'm not really sure. I've never felt intimidated about expressing my opinions, but on the other hand, I have several close Jewish friends I wouldn't want to hurt. Maybe I should answer your question this way. I'm against violence by any country, including the United States and Israel. I'm not afraid to speak out on this issue anywhere, or at any time, or, for that matter, in front of anyone."

"Then perhaps you should begin to speak out against Israel's violence against the Palestinians," he said.

Knowing it would be useless to continue this further, I attempted to change the subject. Although our conversation took a less serious tone during the remainder of the evening, and knowing it was getting late, I decided to ask one more favor.

"Fatiah, if I wanted to talk with a Hezbollah militant, someone who was engaged in the last war, or even violence, would that be possible?"

"I don't get involved in these things." His quick response revealed that he didn't have to think twice about this.

Not ready to give up, I asked, "If I can't meet such a person, then how about a telephone conversation? Is that possible?" I asked, hoping for a breakthrough. Still, Fatiah just continued staring into his glass.

Finally, lifting his glass halfway, he stopped and turned toward me, saying, "Why do you want to involve yourself in such things?"

"As I said, I'm writing a book, and I need to understand. It's important to me," I said in hope of reassuring him.

Fatiah was gripping his glass of beer tightly, as he stared into it. I could tell he was giving it thought.

"If such a thing could be arranged, I want no part of it." Fatiah was looking directly into my eyes, waiting for a response.

"You have my word on it," I said.

"All I can do is ask. That's all. Do you understand? The rest is up to you."

"Agreed. You have my word on it."

Fatiah, instead of using his own phone, used the public one. After several minutes, he returned to the bar. I wondered why he was engaging in all this clandestine behavior. Certainly I wasn't meeting "The Jackal." I only wanted to meet someone in Hezbollah who had fought to resist an Israeli incursion into Lebanon.

"No one can meet you before you leave, but if you want to leave a list of questions with me, he might answer them. No promises, though."

"I understand. Can we move to a booth so I can sit down and make up a list of questions?" Without waiting for an answer, I walked to an empty table and sat down, followed by Fatiah.

Taking out the pen and pad I always carry with me, I began to write down as many questions as I could think of to ask. This was complicated by the fact I'd already had too many beers to drink. Each time I wrote a question on the pad I found myself crossing it out and replacing it with another. After a half hour, I handed the list to Fatiah, who looked over the questions with interest.

"I'll translate them into Arabic. I can tell you now, some of these questions won't be answered, at least not in writing," Fatiah said.

"Well, let's see what happens. When do you think I might be able to get the answers? Don't forget that I have to leave for Israel soon."

"If you get anything back, I'll ask my friend who drives a cab at night to drop off an envelope at the guard booth for you."

We continued to share another two beers together before shaking hands, and I left to return to the marina. The following day, all I could think about was my discussion the evening before with Fatiah.

To my disappointment, no one came the following day. In frustration, I walked to the taxi stand around the corner from the yacht club where I'd first met the driver. Not seeing him there, I attempted to describe him to other drivers. I learned he had just taken a fare into Beirut and would probably return within an hour. After passing time walking the streets, I returned to discover the driver I was looking for still hadn't returned. As I began walking, a cab pulled up. "Are you the American writer, and what's your name?" the taxi driver asked.

"That's me, all right. My name is Ahmed."

"Get in the cab," the driver said.

I entered the cab and we sped away from the Christian part of the city.

"Did you get a response to my list of questions?" I asked.

"Maybe," the driver said, as if he enjoyed teasing me.

"Let's go inside," the driver said, as we parked in front of a pub. Walking into the pub and up to the bar, we both sat to order a beer.

"So, do you have my list?" I asked.

"No, but I have some of the answers to your questions. He wouldn't write anything down. First, you have to promise you won't use my name in anything you write."

"I will change people's names. It's a promise, and you have my word on it."

Because I hadn't made a copy of my questions I asked him to go through my list one question at a time. Removing the list from his jacket pocket, he unfolded it and cleared his throat. He took out a second piece of paper and also unfolded it. "Are those your notes?" I asked.

"I made a few notes so I wouldn't forget," he said, while holding the paper tightly against his chest.

"Question 1. Are you or do you consider yourself a militant who would die for his country?"

"He says he doesn't want to die but is willing to give his life to defend his country."

"Question 2. Were you involved with resisting the Israeli incursion in 2006 and, if you were, did you kill anyone?"

"He says yes and is very proud of that."

"Does 'yes' mean he was involved and killed someone?" I asked.

"I'm not sure," the man responded.

"Question 3. Is Hezbollah involved in the political killings in Lebanon? If your answer is no, then who do you believe is to blame?"

"He says Hezbollah is not involved. He believes that Israel is to blame for these killings to divide Lebanon.

Question 4. Who is responsible today for the Beirut bombings?

"He says it has never been proven who is responsible because no one has ever been caught. He says there are fanatics within every group. He wants to make it clear these bombings are not sanctioned by Hezbollah.

"Question 5. Does Syria provide weapons to Hezbollah in Lebanon?"

"He says Israel gets its weapons of mass destruction from the United States. How else will Hezbollah defend Lebanon without receiving weapons and support from its friends?

"Question 6. Are you an important person in Hezbollah?"

"Sorry, I have no answer to this question," the man sitting next to me said.

"Then, can you answer my question?" I asked

"I said there was no answer to your question," he stated firmly.

"Question 7. How do you view the role of the Christian politicians in Lebanon?

"Most of them are aligned with the United States, who support Israel. America wants to control Lebanon, but we won't allow them to do that. They are traitors to Lebanon."

"Question 8. Does Hezbollah support terrorism?"

"He says your terrorist is his martyr. He says a man who dies for his country to defend it against the aggression of another is an honorable man, not a terrorist."

"And you, my friend. You know what I was asking. Does Hezbollah support terrorism?" I asked the man sitting next to me.

As he took his time to consider his answer, I wasn't at first sure he would respond. "We don't have bombs and airplanes to drop them. Do you think Israel would be talking to the Palestinians if they weren't applying pressure to Israel?"

I had heard this so many times before I had become almost bored with the answer. Rather than continue a discussion that would lead nowhere, I asked instead for him to continue with the list.

"Question 9. How many people belong to Hezbollah in Lebanon, and how many are active and willing to serve in a combat role?"

"He says more than 70 percent of the people in Lebanon support Hezbollah. He says that Hezbollah has willing recruits available when the need is there.

"Is this true?" I asked the man, reading from my list and his list.

"Probably," he responded.

"Question 10. Have you ever committed a terrorist act, and can you tell me in general terms what it consisted of?"

"He says you would have to define a terrorist act before he could answer your question."

"Question 11. What caused you to join Hezbollah?"

"He says because they defend his country. He says if it weren't for Hezbollah then Israel would already occupy Lebanon.

"Question 12. Would you fight for the Palestinian cause?"

"He says everyone in the Middle East fights for the Palestinian cause. He says that Israel will be forced to stop occupying Palestinian lands someday. The Palestinians will have their own country and not be treated like animals."

"Question 13. Do you hate Jews and want an end to the Palestinian State?

"He says he hates the Jews that steal Arab land by building Jewish settlements and invading Palestinian territories and even Lebanon."

"Question 14. How do you see the future of Lebanon and its relationship with Israel?"

He says unless there is a power sharing in Lebanon's parliament that's not based on Christian rule, there is a great danger of another civil war. He says he doesn't feel Israel can be trusted, and only a very strong Lebanon that's united can stand up to the aggressor and its American friends."

"Question 15. Would you be willing to meet with me privately?"

"He says, not this time. He says if you return, then, maybe."

Most of the answers were predictable. Although there was nothing earth-shattering or very revealing, my purpose was to develop a profile for how such a person thought. After a few more beers, I engaged my new friend to get his input and insights into what was happening in Lebanon. Eventually our conversation turned from politics to what he believed were the most important things to the people of Lebanon, Syria, and the other Middle Eastern countries. I took away from his answers the idea that even militants want the same things in life as everyone else, but they use different means to achieve them. Even he wanted his mother to be proud of him and feared she wouldn't. He saw himself as a brave soldier fighting for the just cause of his people. Above all else, he saw himself fighting for and defending Lebanon.

I was left only with the feeling that I could have been talking to any young man anywhere who felt proud to defend his country. In response to my specific questions concerning terrorism, he emphasized that he was not a terrorist, and he and the people he had fought with did not participate in terrorist activities. This reply he repeated several times to similar questions.

At the end of the evening we stood and shook hands. As he attempted to withdraw his hand, I held it tightly. "It's you, isn't it?" I asked.

"How did you know?"

"For starters, the picture in the cab isn't yours. I assumed you borrowed it."

"Very good. And what else did you figure out?" the man asked.

"You're very articulate, so maybe you're important as well," I said, fishing for more details.

"If I was important, why would I come to see you myself?" he said, smiling.

"Maybe you were suspicious and wanted to see for yourself who I was."

"Well then, maybe you're lucky I believe you."

"I'm sure I am." It was now my turn to smile.

"What will you write about us?" he asked.

"I will write about what you've told me, and it will be in your own words."

"That's good," he said, sounding pleased.

"I better head back to the marina; it's getting late."

"I'll have someone drive you back. I want you to be safe."

"Will I be?" I asked, trying to make a joke but seriously wondering if I weren't putting myself at risk.

"My personal driver will take you back. I give you my word; you have no cause to be afraid," were his final words to me.

Although I had no cause to doubt him, I was relieved to arrive back at the marina security gate.

That evening, Helen was invited to hold the American flag and speak briefly during the flag ceremony at the yacht club formal dinner. Because of the recent bombings, it was decided at the last minute it would be safer to hold the dinner and party indoors. When Helen's time came to approach the podium, a hush fell over the entire audience, which was now divided into two parts, separated by a brass railing. One part was Lebanese yacht club members, and the other half was the rally.

As Helen stood at the microphone holding the American flag, her words were brief and to the point, "The American people are with you, and we are working for peace at home."

Everyone smiled, and Helen left the podium. We later learned there had been several more bombings in downtown Beirut that evening.

Knowing we would soon be leaving Lebanon, I could only remember the many people I'd talked to, especially Mary and her children. How different were they, I thought, from any of us who only want security and stability for our own children? When we hear of these places on the evening news, they remain impersonal places, too far away for us to fully understand what's happening in these countries.

We're encouraged to support one country, the country that represents our own politics and political interests. Rarely are efforts made to help us understand life in these countries or to understand how, through encouraging global empathy, the news media could promote changing the world and ultimately promote enduring and lasting peace.

My thoughts are with the suffering Lebanese people as they continue their struggle to preserve their fragile democracy.

CHAPTER 10

▼

GATEWAY TO ISRAEL

We had never visited Israel and the Holy Land. A land between Egypt and Meso-potamia, it is home to three of the world's major religions: Judaism (sixth century BC), Christianity (first century AD), and Islamism (seventh century AD). After a war of independence in 1948, it emerged as a Jewish state, following a United Nations truce that was accepted by both Israel and its five Arab neighbors. From that day until now, Israel continues to be under siege from some of its neighbors, including the Palestinians.

On this evening, we left for Haifa, Israel, one of three ports we would be visit-ing in Israel. Haifa is home to two universities and Israel's third major port. We were provided precise entry positions (gates) for entering Israeli waters, secret codes for emergencies, and several other specific instructions to guarantee our safe entry.

During darkness, we were approached by Israeli gunboats, which identified the captain, yacht details, and certified the Eastern Mediterranean Rally number of our yacht displayed on the bow rail. Because of these precautions, it would have been difficult for a terrorist to enter Israeli waters under the umbrella of a rally yacht. Before sunrise, Israeli military jets flew above us without lights and probably using infrared cameras.

In the morning, each of us was escorted one by one into the marina, followed by a military inflatable with a manned machine gun on the bow. Once inside the breakwater, we were approached by another vessel, asked specific questions, and requested to place our passports into a handheld net for inspection. When this procedure was completed, we were given permission one by one to enter the marina and tie off. Israeli customs and immigration officials came to each boat to collect passports and request specific information about the boat and crew. At all times, everyone was courteous and helpful and made us feel welcome to Israel.

We were guests of the Carmel Yacht Club, which had arranged for our entry. In Haifa, we enjoyed tours of Haifa and Bahia Garden, and a full-day tour to Galilee, including Nazareth. Although I am as interested in Muslim holy sites as Christian ones, there appeared to be an emphasis upon Christian sites by our guides.

The Carmel Yacht Club gave a cocktail party and buffet dinner, which was an excellent opportunity to meet members of the club and begin to develop a sense of Israel. A retired rear admiral of the Israeli navy and member of the yacht club welcomed us formally to Israel. He was a delightful and interesting man, who loved to dance and party as much as the rest of us. Although wanting to discuss and exchange views with him, I saw him besieged by others hoping to get to know him better.

On the second evening, those interested were given the opportunity to spend an evening with an Israeli family in their home. There were six of us invited to the home of a yacht club member, a young chemical engineer. Here, we enjoyed a wonderful dinner and met his wife and young children. They described to us how, only a year before, they had stood on their roof and watched rockets rain down on the city.

Although most of us avoided political discussions, a young American-Jewish woman raised the subject of Lebanon. She described how Hezbollah had won the hearts of the people because of their good works there.

Our host stopped, thought for a minute, and said, "I hate to say this, but you're naive. They get their money from Iran, and they buy the hearts of the people." He went on, "Israel was doing the job of the Lebanese government by fighting terrorists and Hezbollah." He added, "The Lebanese know they are safe."

I remembered Mary from Lebanon and wished that this man's wife and Mary could spend time together, discussing not only their differences but how to bridge the gap between both countries. At the risk of sounding overly simplistic, I still had little doubt that both women could come to an understanding and maybe find a solution to their nations' problems.

The following day, it was time to leave for the eighty-five-nautical-mile overnight journey from Haifa to Ashkelon, Israel. Again, we were provided specific waypoints by the Israeli navy, which the rally directors admonished us to strictly adhere to. We arrived at the Ashkelon Marina, a modern one with all amenities. The city of Ashkelon is also known as The Garden City, and is a popular recreational and tourist resort with many beautiful white sandy beaches.

As was the custom in each country visited, prearranged tours were available to all those who were interested. In Ashkelon, we visited Masada and the Dead Sea, including lunch at a kibbutz. Masada is the fortress where King Herod and his Jewish settlers made a last stand against the Romans. Rather than surrender, they chose death.

A common saying today in Israel is, "Masada will never fall again."

While we walked through the ruins on the top of Masada, we began to hear loud explosions in the far-off distance. One of us commented that these sounded like artillery and bombs.

Returning to the Ashkelon Marina, we heard more explosions, now louder than ever, which continued throughout the night. Someone heard on the BBC that Palestinian political factions, Hammas, and the Fatah party were in an all-out fight to take control of Gaza. We were horrified to think that while we were enjoying ourselves people were dying.

Over the next few days, we continued to hear the sounds of war some twenty kilometers away. Although the Gaza Strip was only fifty kilometers long by six kilometers wide, it was one of the world's oldest towns, well established by 2000 BC. It's said that Gaza has been conquered and destroyed more times than any other city in the world.

Most sailors, because of their interest in the world, follow current events. We had all placed our hopes in a peaceful coexistence between Hammas, an extremist organization, and Fatah, a political entity willing to recognize and negotiate with Israel. When we heard that Hammas had forcibly taken Gaza, most of us lost hope for a peaceful settlement with Israel in the near future.

The morning after we returned to the marina, a number of us gathered on the dock to discuss recent events. With the sound of exploding shells in the background, a conversation ensued when one person said to another, "There will never be peace now."

"Why not?" I asked.

"Isn't it obvious?" he said. Without waiting for me to respond, he continued, saying, "Because Hammas refuses to recognize Israel and resorts to using violence, so Israel won't negotiate with them."

"Maybe, but then, what good is a peace agreement when it doesn't include everyone? If Hammas represents a significant portion of the Palestinians and if Israel isn't forced to directly deal with its most extreme adversary, how will a lasting peace ever be negotiated? Wouldn't a peace agreement with only Fatah be limited? Remember, although Fatah represents a much greater land mass, they represent less than half the Palestinians. On the other hand, an agreement that included Hammas and Fatah could result in an all-inclusive peace settlement and creation of a Palestinian state."

"They are still terrorists, and how can you trust terrorists?" he asked me.

"While I personally regard Hammas as a terrorist organization, I've always believed that diplomacy and talking face-to-face with your enemy is the only way to reach common ground, and in Israel's case, this could mean peace."

"You're naive!" he said.

"Maybe," I answered.

As he walked away, I could tell he was upset with me.

Considering the last few days, we were all upset. Hearing the explosion of artillery in the background gave us little hope that things there would ever improve. Because we had visited North Cyprus, Syria, Lebanon, and now Israel, we felt a vested interest in each country's future. Something appeared to be happening to all of us on the rally. We had become sympathetic and begun to bond with, not just one country at the expense of another, but with the people of all countries. Meeting average people on the street was beginning to have an impact on each of us.

Not long afterward I heard the unverifiable rumor that the Turkish coast guard was in international waters, prepared to escort us back to North Cyprus if required. Although it was never confirmed, I preferred to believe that this was the case. I knew many Turkish coast guard officers were trained at the U.S. Coast Guard Academy and spoke English. Unlike most third-world countries, Turkey didn't rely upon used U.S. Navy cutters but, instead, purchased the newest and latest equipment for patrolling its waters.

We did make a trip to the Dead Sea and enjoyed lunch at another kibbutz. I knew that in the beginning the kibbutz was an important part of Israeli defense and represented a socialist lifestyle that today has largely changed with the times in order to survive. Although some kibbutzim still enjoy a simple lifestyle, many have found new ways to survive economically, including the construction of hotels and conference centers, and have become centers of big business.

Because the kibbutz on the Dead Sea was crowded, we elected to first put on our bathing suits and swim in the Dead Sea before lunch. A building near the water's edge provided a place to change our clothes and cost one shekel. Helen locked her clothes inside a locker provided for this purpose. After swimming, we returned to the building to discover that, for Helen to reclaim her clothes, she had to pay another shekel, regardless of the fact that she didn't have change. Another tourist took pity and gave Helen the shekel necessary to reclaim her clothing.

While I waited outside for Helen, I saw three elderly Muslim women sitting in the shade. One woman reached over to take a garden hose and wash her feet. A young woman with tattoos stormed toward her, took the hose away and admonished the woman. I felt embarrassed for them as they stood and walked away.

CHAPTER 11

▼

PORT SAID, EGYPT

We looked forward to visiting Port Said, located at the northern end of the Suez Canal, which links the Mediterranean to the Red Sea. In Port Said, large container ships gather before they convoy through the canal. Egypt, once under the leadership of Gamal Abdel Nasser, was the first Middle Eastern country to break away from the United Arab countries to make a lasting peace with Israel. Although ostracized by his Arab neighbors for these actions, he single-handedly reintroduced a sense of pride among Egyptians, which had been absent for almost 450 years. After his assassination, he was replaced by President Hosni Mubarek, who carried on most of his policies and close association with the West.

Another overnight trip and 124 nautical miles later, we arrived in Port Said, Egypt. Although we weren't excited about returning to Egypt, we did so because Jackie hadn't been to Cairo. Arriving at the predetermined location just outside the Suez Canal, we began circling in preparation for entering the canal. Because of the heat and congestion, tempers began to flare over the VHF radio.

Our organizer, Hassan, in a way that only he could manage, defused the situation with just a few words, saying with a Turkish accent, "I know everyone is hot and tired, but soon we will be in the marina and can relax."

And then he began to sing a few words of a song over the VHF radio. The situation was defused, and once again, everyone began to cooperate in the spirit and camaraderie we had all become used to.

Each of us dressed our yachts in colorful signal flags from the top of the mast to the foredeck and aft. The canal was briefly closed, and we formed a procession into the canal, led by a pilot boat. We entered the Egyptian naval basin and anchored along the quay. Armed navy personnel were assigned night and day to protect our yachts and were stationed every few hundred feet. At the entrance to the base, there were two truckloads of soldiers with rifles ready at all times. Temporary electrical panels were set up, each wired to the one before it. They were so overloaded that barely a few minutes went by without one of us blowing a circuit. Because my power cord wasn't long enough to reach the panel, I got a local fellow to go into town and purchase the necessary longer power cord to reach the electrical board. When he returned, I was informed the cord and ends would cost me US$160. After putting the ends on the cord, I proceeded to connect *Tahlequah* to the power board. Each time I attempted this, I proceeded to blow out everyone's power. Removing the plug end, I saw it had shorted out. Fortunately, I had a spare below and was able to remedy the problem. Because there were so few amps available, I gave up trying to use our air conditioner.

While I busied myself with boat projects, Jackie and Helen went into town. Although forewarned by the rally organizers, Helen forgot and wore shorts. As most women in Port Said wear full black burkas, Helen, with her bare legs, stood out from everyone. A cab driver began giving Helen more attention than she wanted, and because of the distraction, the cab driver hit a parked car. His bent hood flew up, and the headlight glass went flying in all directions. Jackie and Helen made a speedy retreat back to the naval base.

Whenever we left the base, armed naval personnel were assigned to accompany us through the streets. Accepting a pack of cigarettes, our guard agreed to leave us on our own. We were then able to talk to people on the street without fear of intimidation and censorship. On the street, most Egyptians took us for English and frequently attempted to engage us in hope of enticing us to purchase something from them.

One shopkeeper had a unique and different approach. He said to us, "We have the same junk as everybody else. Come in take a look at my trash, and I'll give you a good price if you see something you like."

His approach did get me to stop and laugh. Because his English was as good as mine, we stopped long enough to discuss where we were from, how long we had been in Egypt, and other unimportant things. As all shopkeepers do, he offered Helen and me a cup of tea, which we felt obliged to accept, lest we insult him. As we sat down at the back of his shop, he began the usual attempt at interesting us in his junk.

"You know, I'm not going to buy any of this stuff, but I would like to just sit and talk."

"At least you are honest," said the shopkeeper.

After explaining to him that I was working on a book and interested in learning more about how Westerners are thought of in this part of the world, I said, "So tell me, truthfully, how do Egyptians really feel about Americans?"

"Honestly?" he said.

"Yes, honestly," I responded.

"No one will tell you this, but Americans aren't thought of too highly here."

"And why?" I asked.

"Hmmm," the shopkeeper hesitated. "Well, for one thing, people here believe America declared a war on Muslims."

"Really?" I said, in an effort to encourage him to go further.

"Maybe not a war, but it's commonly believed that Muslims aren't liked in America. Some of my friends have relatives in America, and they tell me people fear Muslims there." He looked a little uncomfortable at criticizing America in front of an American. "You asked, so I'm telling you," the shopkeeper added.

"I don't think most Americans know any Muslims," I felt obliged to say.

"Do you fear Muslims in the United States?" he asked.

"No, of course not," I said, attempting to leave no doubt of my feelings. Of course, I knew exactly what he was talking about. I knew if I were a Muslim in the United States, I would certainly feel under suspicion.

"I've read in the newspaper that Muslims in America used to generously donate money to Muslim charities here in Egypt and elsewhere. But because the FBI now investigates all donations to Muslim charities, many have stopped doing this in fear of being under suspicion by the American government. Do you think this is fair?" the shopkeeper asked.

"I think that all money leaving the States is investigated, according to my American bank. When I bought property and had to transfer money outside the country, I was informed by my bank I had to be in the United States to make such a transfer at the time, and it might have to be reported. So, as far as I know, it may not only be Muslims," I said.

"I traveled to America a few years ago, and your immigration people hassled me when I entered. They pulled me out of line and took me to a back room and began asking me a lot of questions. I felt it was because my wife wore a headscarf. They weren't polite either—you would not be treated like that in my country."

I couldn't help but think to myself that Egyptian customs and immigration might be polite, but that it was still a police state.

"I understand how you feel about your treatment entering the United States. Even Americans complain about being mistreated. I know personally how rude they can be."

I knew exactly what the shopkeeper was talking about. I had personally had several experiences and had some of my European friends tell me they refused to even change planes in the United States because of how rude immigration workers had been to them.

"Are tourists safe in Egypt?" I asked.

"I know there have been several large-scale attacks on tourists over the years, but they are few and far between, and, personally, I don't believe the people responsible are even Egyptians."

"So why do I see army trucks and machine gun emplacements at intersections and military escorts for tourist buses traveling together to go to Luxor and Cairo?" I asked.

"Oh, that. That's only to make tourists feel safe. The government wants tourists to feel the government is doing something to protect them, so they don't have to worry," he said confidently, as if he knew the answer.

I knew better than this. Tourism had suffered in Egypt ever since sixty tourists had died in a terrorist attack in 1997. Even recently, there had been smaller-scale attacks on foreigners. Egypt is a different type of democracy and not one that totally respects civil rights. News columnists, people from political parties, and others have been arrested and incarcerated for little more than sharing opinions that didn't have government approval. In addition, the government prohibits unsanctioned demonstrations of any kind, considering them to be the cause of civil disturbance and unrest. At busy intersections I've encountered machine gun emplacements behind sandbags with more armed soldiers nearby. Even Mubarek's political challengers have faced charges resulting in arrest and prison sentences. No opposition candidate can challenge Mubarek unless personally approved by his party. In other words, there are few successful political challenges.

It must be recognized that Egypt is one of the few countries in the Middle East that recognizes Israel's existence and enjoys a good working relationship with them. Egypt has helped broker peace in the region for many years and continues to do so. Egypt walks a fine line between being an ally of the United States and an ally of its neighbors, some of whom envision a different world order in the Middle East.

"If I were to ask you what you would like Americans to know about Egyptians, what would you say?"

"We're your friends. Come and see Egypt—it's a beautiful country and the people are friendly. What do you like about Egypt?" the shopkeeper asked.

"What do I like…. Well, I like the antiquities, of course. I like the narrow side streets with the shops and vendors. I like the many bazaars and markets. I suppose I like a lot about Egypt," I said, hoping to hide the fact that sometimes the pesky street peddlers drove me crazy.

"What don't you like about Egypt?" he asked.

Although uncomfortable with the question, I decided I owed him honesty. "I don't like baksheesh; it drives me up a wall."

"Do you understand what baksheesh is?" he asked.

"I suppose it's begging."

"In some ways, yes, and in other ways, it isn't. You see, baksheesh teaches us humility. The Koran requires even a child from a wealthy family to go into the street and beg so he will learn humility. And that is the origin of baksheesh."

Although in theory I admired the intention, I also knew baksheesh had been misused as a means of demanding a tip for things as simple as asking a question of someone on the street.

Feeling that I had taken our conversation as far as I could, I said, "My wife and I have promised to be back before 4:00, so we have to leave, but I want to thank you for talking to me."

"You won't use my name?" the shopkeeper asked.

"No, of course not. Especially if you don't want me to," I said, realizing I'd already forgotten it!

A few years before, while staying in a hotel on a tour to Luxor, I had returned to the hotel late one evening. As I exited the elevator, a man stationed there rushed to the opened door of my room. Walking to my room, I remained outside in the hallway, demanding to know what the five men, all dressed in suits, were doing in my room.

In perfect English, I was told, "Sorry, we don't speak English."

Protesting this to the hotel manager, I was given the lame excuse that he had allowed five tour agents to see my room. Informing him that I didn't accept his explanation that five tour agents were inspecting my room at midnight, I demanded he bring the police to the hotel immediately so a report could be made. The manager then informed me that if he did this, he would be fired immediately, and he begged me to drop the whole thing. Reluctantly, I decided to dispense with the police but did call another couple in the hotel to inform them of what had happened and ask them to be sure I showed up for breakfast in the morning.

Later that evening I discovered that someone had gone through my briefcase. Inside was a printed copy of a book I was working on. The numbered pages were now out of order and, strangely, a few pages were missing. My laptop was plugged in and left on the dresser with the password screen still on. I can only assume I interrupted someone trying to access my laptop. There was little doubt that the men in my room were secret police and there to conduct a random search—something I believe happens frequently in Egypt. Before going to sleep I put the spare single bed in front of the door to prevent it from being easily opened and a glass on the doorknob. I was determined not to be surprised, and I needed a good night's rest.

The following morning, when the tour guide arrived in the lobby, he angrily made a fuss to the hotel manager, saying "If you treat your guests and my customers this way, I won't return. There are other hotels I can take my customers to."

Routinely, when we boarded buses to travel to other areas, armed men in suits were put on the bus to protect or maybe keep a watchful eye over us.

Once again, Jackie and Helen ventured into town alone, this time suitably covered. A bakery offered Jackie and Helen a delicious-tasting bread stick, filled with a fig compote. They bought a bagful; after they returned home they discovered the ones they had bought didn't have a filling! Our experiences in Egypt, past and present, are full of anecdotes like these.

The next day, Jackie and 95 percent of the rally participants left on a two-day tour to Cairo. Because Helen and I had previously done these tours, it was our intention to find a nice local hotel and escape boat life for a few days. It was then that we learned there was a sporting event in town, and no hotel rooms were available at any price. Although disappointed, we accepted our situation and made the best of it. I used our unexpected extra time to perform several repairs aboard *Tahlequah*.

Dave (*SV Mashona*) came to *Tahlequah* to thank me for giving him a copy of my last book. As he began to walk up the plank, it suddenly folded, dumping him into the drink. Hearing Helen's blood-curdling scream, I rushed to the cockpit. Looking over the side, I could see David's shocked expression, as he dog-paddled to stay afloat.

Pulling himself from the water on a neighbor's ladder, he said, "They set a trap for me."

As usual, David was a good sport, and we all laughed about it later—not to mention, we gave him three gin and tonics for breakfast!

That evening, I decided to return to town and see if I couldn't find another shopkeeper to talk with. As I passed the shop where I'd talked with the shopkeeper only the day before, he rushed out to greet me.

"Come in and have tea with me," the shopkeeper said excitedly.

Knowing better than to refuse a cup of tea, I accepted his offer, as I typically do when offered one. After we had discussed many things, the shopkeeper asked if I'd ever smoked a water pipe. When I'd admitted I enjoyed apple tobacco, he proceeded to search his shelf for some.

"Found some!" he suddenly cried out. "Come with me, and we'll sit in the back of the shop."

While loading the metal cup of the pipe intended for me, he looked up. "Would you like something stronger?" the shopkeeper said, smiling.

"No, thanks. I'll stick with the apple. Thanks."

Hearing this, the shopkeeper finished loading the metal cup, placed a small piece of tinfoil on top, and then the charcoal. After filling the glass vase halfway with water, he lit the charcoal, and took a couple puffs before handing the mouthpiece to me.

"Here, try this," he said. The shopkeeper then began to unwrap his own personal stash before repeating the same procedure.

Sitting there on low wooden stools, we began to smoke our water pipes. Each time he breathed in, he held his breath for a few seconds before exhaling with a sigh of satisfaction. I was trying to avoid breathing his secondhand smoke, knowing I still had to find my way back to the naval base at the end of the evening. I could tell the hashish was taking its toll on the shopkeeper. As time went on, his eyes began to develop a glassy look, and his words sounded different, but not slurred.

If I were going to ask questions, this seemed the appropriate time to do it. "Can I ask you a few questions about life here in Egypt?" I said.

"Yes ... yes, my friend. You can ask me anything. We are brothers who smoke together now. We are friends; friends can ask each other anything," the shopkeeper said.

Maybe from the secondhand smoke, even I was beginning to feel relaxed and felt I could ask anything of the shopkeeper. "Are all women circumcised in Egypt?" I asked.

"Who would marry a woman who wasn't circumcised?" the shopkeeper asked.

"I guess I would," I said, as we both began to laugh.

"Yes, my friend, but you are not a good Muslim."

"Do you have daughters, and were they circumcised?" I asked.

"Oh, yes, of course. All young girls are circumcised. But I have a secret."

"What is your secret?" I inquisitively asked.

"You must promise you will never tell on your brother."

"I promise I will never reveal your name or who you are. How's that?" I asked.

"If you tell, I will have to kill you."

"Okay, so tell me," I said, now more curious than ever.

"I didn't really have my daughters circumcised. No, I didn't do that to them." The shopkeeper said this in a way that revealed he was still keeping something back.

"What did you do?" I asked.

"What many do today. The girls are just nicked. That way, we can claim they were circumcised."

"Do many do that?" I asked.

"Some do, but some don't." He sighed again while exhaling his water pipe. "People don't talk too much about what they do to their daughters. Backward people still do it, but the government is educating people. Even some mullahs say this is not in the Koran. Better to nick them; then everybody is happy."

"Do people in Egypt practice mercy killing?" I asked.

"Nobody talks about such things. When someone dies in a family, it's the family's business, nobody else's." The shopkeeper's eyes were beginning to roll.

"Can I put you into a cab to get home?" I asked.

"No, my son comes to get me every night at this time."

After thanking the shopkeeper, I stood to rise. The shopkeeper was having difficulty rising; he grabbed me with both hands, saying, "My brother, you must come back again. Promise me that you will come back."

"I'll do what I can."

With those words, I made it out the door and walked back to the marina.

We continued to receive reports the Palestinians were fighting, and we wondered if it would be possible for us to visit Jerusalem when we returned to Israel for our final get-together and party. The next day Jackie returned, saying that everyone had had a wonderful time in Cairo, seeing the Cairo museum, pyramids, and sphinx.

The following morning, we left Port Said once again in procession with the ship dressed. We began our final 136-nautical-mile leg of the rally to Herzliya, Israel. We cooperated again with the Israeli navy, respecting their many requirements for entry into Israeli waters. A navy gunboat met us at their territorial waters and accompanied us to the marina and remained there during our entire stay. Herzliya Marina is a very modern marina with all amenities, including shopping mall, theater, full supermarket, and many enjoyable restaurants. Herzliya is located only five nautical miles from the city of Tel Aviv.

Our first tour was to visit the city of Jerusalem. En route to Jerusalem we drove through the West Bank. Our driver was keen to point out that one or two of the homes on the slopes of the West Bank were middle class, making the point that the Palestinians didn't want people from the Gaza Strip coming there to live. Although not sure how he came to this conclusion, I took note of the point he wanted to make.

Traversing the West Bank, I saw signs of newly constructed Jewish settlements fenced off with special concrete structures—we were told it was to protect them from rocket attack. The driver emphasized that, without these fences, there would be many more attacks upon Israeli citizens. We saw miles of fences intended to restrict the movement of people crossing into Israel.

Jerusalem is a remarkable city with many holy sites important to Jewish, Christian, and Muslim pilgrims. We began our tour by walking the narrow streets of the old part of the city, where there were hundreds of shops. On one street winding its way up a hill are the Stations of the Cross, where Jesus walked on his way to crucifixion. We saw eight stations with signs describing which station we were passing. Secretly, I wondered how people could know the exact spot where Veronica wiped Jesus's brow or another helped Jesus up to continue his ordeal. More important was the fact that people came here on a Christian pilgrimage to follow the example of Jesus. Some stations had small chapels, one had a nunnery, and some only had small signs designating the station of the cross. The hundreds of shops along the route Jesus walked were selling religious items of all kinds.

We then visited the oldest part of the city and the Western (Wailing) Wall. The wall itself is the last remaining remnant of the temple built by King Solomon in 950 BC. Entering this square, we first had to pass through another perimeter of security and have our packages, backpacks, and pocketbooks carefully scanned and, in some cases, searched.

Standing near the wall, our guide told us of how, during the 1967 Six-Day War, he had been a soldier in the Israeli army. During the conflict, they had fought to regain Jerusalem.

As he stood at the Western Wall, he described another soldier saying, "Do you realize we've fought two thousand years for this wall?" He said this with a sense of pride, his eyes filling with tears.

Although I can appreciate what this wall represents, I thought silently, *why did so many people on both sides have to die for a wall?*

There were many bar mitzvahs happening in the square. While the men and women were separated by a partition, the women stood on benches and chairs beside the wall separating the sexes in order to throw flowers to their children. Helen moved to join the women throwing flowers. It was clearly a momentous time in their lives, for the men, women, and children, and was a proud memory they would cherish always. I saw groups of men blowing large horns, as well as groups of men parading through the square holding very large Torahs. I saw groups of Hasidic Jews singing holy verses together. Clearly, this was a place that symbolized the essence of Judaism.

I saw a large family of several generations. Suddenly, the eldest, a short man in his late seventies, began to dance in front of the others. Watching his face and the faces of the others, I saw something rare that defied description but nonetheless was present, and his family clearly saw it. With his hands raised into the air, he began to move first in one direction and then the other, as his family clapped and sang a song in Hebrew. It was an infectious melody that swept everyone up into the emotion it created for the family and those standing nearby. I was struck by his importance to the others and how his aged appearance suddenly gave way to a youthful rebirth that shone through his face and graceful movements. What I witnessed was a spontaneous spiritual occurrence that a man experiences rarely in his lifetime and one I felt privileged to see.

I saw young Israeli soldiers, both men and women, carrying automatic rifles and backpacks. Soldiers walked public squares, narrow, winding streets, and generally could be found in any public area. Even when out of uniform they carried their weapons into shopping malls, theaters, and restaurants. Because many of the soldiers were only eighteen, I frequently did a double take because they appeared to be so young.

One afternoon, sitting in a kosher McDonald's, we saw about thirty young soldiers come in. The first thing we noticed is that they wore their pants in the same way young people typically do. Their trousers hung down, baggy style, below their waists. Not expecting this, we were surprised to see their fashion statement was tolerated by the military.

Our guide brought us to the Holy Church of the Sepulcher, the tomb of Christ. Helen, the mother of Constantine, declared that anyone who found the cross of Christ would be cured of all ailments. A woman reputably discovered the cross on the exact spot where today the Holy Church of the Sepulcher is constructed. To commemorate the spot where the cross was discovered, Helen built the first structure there. It has been modified and added to many times during the centuries. Once again, it seemed less important to me that this was actually the tomb of Christ and more important that it represented something special to Christians.

As we entered the church, it became apparent that five different Christian sects had staked their claim in the church and occupied different areas of it. The Greek Orthodox represents the "law of the church" and is responsible for making any formal decisions. During our tour, we saw many people kneeling and kissing the granite cover to Christ's tomb. Because the different Christian sects continuously squabbled within the church, a local Muslim family was chosen five hundred years ago to guard and protect the keys to the Church. For five hundred years, a member of this family each day has opened and closed the church with the same key. No one is allowed to remain overnight.

We drove to the outskirts of Jerusalem to have lunch at another kibbutz. Following lunch, the guide took us to a scenic overlook. From there we saw Bethlehem in the distance. There was a fence that separated Israel from its neighboring Muslim village. Our guide stated that world criticism was based upon misinformation, because these walls were constructed between Israeli and neighboring towns and were not constructed along Israel's entire border. I began to get a sense, not only from our guide, but from the several Israelis we encountered, that they were sensitive to world opinion and criticism. They used each opportunity to defend their country's actions both at home and abroad and wanted us to understand what life was like in Israel living with the ongoing threat of armed conflict and terrorism. Silently, I recalled President Carter's words comparing the treatment of the Palestinians to apartheid in South Africa.

CHAPTER 12

▼

END OF THE RALLY: REFLECTIONS ON ISRAEL

After lunch, Helen and I reminded our guide we had arranged to leave the tour and remain in Jerusalem overnight. Apparently, this had been overlooked. The guide instructed us to get off the tour bus and wait curbside for the #7 local bus that would take us directly past the hotel. We did board the #7 bus, and after a short time we were instructed by the driver to get off and walk about a mile down the road. It was then that we noticed that many streets had been closed by the police using barriers. We were informed that there would be a gay rights march, and the Hasidic Jews were expected to counterdemonstrate. It was the intention of the police to separate both groups for the purpose of preventing a reoccurrence of violence as in years past. We found ourselves in large groups of Hasidic Jews, military, and city police. Asking directions to the hotel only brought blank stares, as no one seemed to know of the hotel.

We eventually found a cab whose driver, with great difficulty, drove us across town, letting us off in front of a hotel whose name was in Hebrew. In the lobby, we were informed that we were at the wrong hotel and would have to go back to the other side of town. Apparently, our tour guide had given us the wrong name of the hotel. The hotel manager suggested we walk another mile in an effort to avoid the demonstrators. Eventually, we did find a cabbie who managed to find an open street through police barriers to take us to the right hotel. We had requested a hotel near Old Jerusalem so we could walk the streets but were surprised to discover our hotel was outside of town. We accepted our plight and made the best of our situation by having a wonderful dinner and watching *CNN News* that evening.

The cost of staying in this five-star hotel was US$80 and included both breakfast and a delightful dinner. Again, there were many soldiers in civilian clothing on the buffet line, with automatic rifles slung over their shoulders. Walking through the hotel promenade earlier, we had seen elderly Hasidic Jews also wearing sidearms. We made the assumption that they lived in West Bank settlements and wore sidearms to protect themselves. Seeing this reminded me of being in South Africa years before. Although I was saddened to see many firearms, everyone seemed to accept this as a normal way of life.

After a good meal and good night's sleep, the next morning we went to Tel Aviv by bus and visited the Tel Aviv Museum of Art. Although the museum was small, it was wonderful. Here Helen bought a book with black-and-white photos taken by a young Israeli woman, depicting the several generations of her family. More importantly, the pictures displayed the many differences within the family and the different lifestyles they had chosen to live. One picture showed three elderly sisters with consecutive tattooed numbers on the forearms from the Nazi death camps. Leaving the museum, we flagged down a cab and took a thirty-minute drive back to the marina.

That evening was the final formal dinner to mark the official end of the Eastern Mediterranean Rally. The dinner was held outside, and there appeared to be more guests than had been invited. Because of this, there was a shortage of tables and chairs for guests, and some last-minute shuffling had to be done to accommodate these people. Hassan gave the closing speech, and it was one to be remembered. He talked about how as individuals we can't change the world, but how as individuals we *can* each return home to present what we've seen and learned in these many countries. He talked about how the mayors in Syria, Lebanon, and Israel each had expressed their heartfelt desire for peace. Only Hassan could get away with saying that as sailors we had learned that Port Said was not to be thought of as just a dirty city, that Israel was not to be thought of as just an aggressive country, Syria was not to be thought of as just a country that threatened the world, and he shared thoughts about Lebanon. Although each of us smiled, we understood Hassan's comments and acknowledged his bravery in sharing his opinions in such a sensitive and open manner. Hassan wanted each of us to learn before the end of the rally that there was much more to the people and countries we visited than what we knew from the news media. Hassan was an ambassador of goodwill, and his goal was to encourage each of us to be the same. His point was well-taken.

Everyone coming into contact with Hassan and David understood that they were dealing with men of integrity and honor and, because of this, kept an open mind to their comments. I understood that Hassan was looking to retire from the rally and wondered whether without his stewardship the rally would continue to survive in the coming years. Hassan left to return to Turkey on June 21, one day after the closing ceremony and dinner in Herzliya, Israel.

This year, we had been informed that the rally would not sponsor the trip to Petra, Jordan, because of lengthy delays experienced the previous year upon return at the Jordanian-Israeli border. Although this meant little to us at the time, we would soon understand fully the implications of what the rally organizers were talking about. Because of this, the rally members organized their own tour. Because Helen and I had previously visited Petra, we elected instead to remain in the marina.

Two years prior, Helen and I had spent time touring and seeing Jordan extensively. We had hired a professor of history to introduce us to Jordan. A country of 5.5 million people, it is bordered by Israel, Syria, Iraq, and Saudi Arabia. It has for many years walked a tightrope between the United States and its Arab neighbors. It was the second country, after Egypt, to recognize and make peace with Israel.

I had always regarded King Hussein, who reigned from 1952 to 1999, as one of the world's great statesmen, whose vision for the future of his country was a remarkable one, considering the times. Even today, his influence as a libertarian is felt with the many freedoms Jordanians enjoy, including freedoms for women.

I once sat in a Bedouin tent in the desert, and we discussed King Hussein and what he meant to the Jordanian people. Even the Bedouins owed their allegiance to King Hussein and today see him as one of the world's great leaders, who ushered Jordan into an era of peace and Western modernization. Once, when we were on a tour of Mount Nebo, a tourist bus arrived, and approximately fifty Jewish business men disembarked. Surprised, I asked my host if this was normal in Jordan.

"Why shouldn't it be normal?" he asked, surprised I would ask such a question. "These people are our friends and our neighbors," he went on to explain.

When I think of the Jordanian people, I always remember that experience.

We were pleased that Jackie would take the four-day trip to Petra and the ancient Arabic kingdom from the fourth century BC. Petra was the city in the film, *Indiana Jones and the Temple of Doom*, and it was a place that one had to visit firsthand to fully appreciate.

Four days later Jackie returned, angered at the way she had been treated by Israeli customs and immigration at the Israeli-Jordanian border. Although Jackie was one of thirty rally people who traveled together, she was the last person within the group to pass through security.

When asked if she had ever been to Lebanon, of course, she said yes. She was then separated from the others, who waited outside on the tour bus. During the next two hours, Jackie was subjected to intense questioning and strip-searched in a private room by a female security guard.

Although told by security that the bus should leave without Jackie, the others refused to do so, saying they had come together, and they would leave together. At hearing this, Israeli security attempted to convince Jackie to influence them to leave. She refused, and the standoff continued. Losing patience, those on the bus demanded to see someone in authority but could find no one over the age of eighteen in charge. A spokesperson for the bus group attempted to explain that we were yachtsman traveling together, we had all been to Syria and Lebanon, and, most importantly, were guests of the Israeli navy. Convincing customs and immigration to contact the Israeli navy was fruitless. Two hours later, Jackie was handed back her passport and given official permission to enter back into Israel—without explanation.

The following morning, I went with Jackie to see customs and immigration officials stationed at the Herzliya Marina. They were already aware of the incident and were upset at what had happened. We were told that a senior customs and immigration official would contact the border-crossing station to discuss the circumstances. Knowing that the same thing had happened the year before, I was doubtful anyone truly cared.

I now believed I understood why—because of border delays the previous year—the rally organizers had refused to officially sponsor or arrange the trip to Petra, Jordan, this year. I suggested Jackie write them to make them aware of the situation; perhaps in future years, trips to Petra, Jordan, could be made from Egypt instead of Israel.

People I spoke with about what had happened were equally incensed over Jackie's treatment. This one incident appeared to overshadow our positive experiences and resulted in some people expressing anger. Two rally participants described how similar things had happened to their daughters when they were traveling alone to Israel. An irate Norwegian captain described how his wife had been detained by Israeli immigration for no other reason than that she had been born in Pakistan. When they attempted to separate her from the line and interrogate her in a back room, her husband insisted on remaining with her. When they informed the officials that they were both Norwegian citizens and wanted the Norwegian embassy involved, Israeli immigration backed down and allowed her to board the plane.

My feelings about Israel were muddled and confused. Having lived in New York for several years, I expected Israel would be much the same, but it was far different. Everything we did was overshadowed by the military—a fact of life in Israel. I began to feel guilty that I was not giving Israel the benefit of the doubt and needed to look harder beneath the surface. My closest friends in life were a Jewish family living in South Africa. The man had met his wife in a kibbutz in Israel in the 1970s and returned there on occasion. I began to feel I was even letting them down.

As an American, there is a part of me that says we must always support Israel. As a global citizen, there is a part of me that says we must be open to the needs of all peoples everywhere and be willing to negotiate and discuss those needs without abandoning our friends. As an American, I want to believe such political openhandedness would benefit Israel and its neighbors in a far more healthy way than our present policies.

Just as I was feeling I hadn't met someone with whom I could share an open discussion about Israel, my prayers were answered. Finally, I met a man with whom I could exchange views and opinions openly. I was in search of a counterpart to the shopkeeper I had talked to in Syria, and Mary, the mother of two children in Lebanon. It was my goal to leave Israel with a balance of ideas and opinions that somehow complemented one another, in my quest to form a better understanding of how people saw their political futures unfolding in today's confused world. Until now, I had found it difficult (not impossible) to discuss certain subjects without making others defensive and sometimes creating the impression by my questions that I was anti-Israeli.

The man I met was involved in the peace movement in Israel and believed that Israel's future depended upon, not the elimination of military actions, but, instead, the emphasis upon diplomacy and peace initiatives. He believed there had been a recent shift to military solutions and that peace initiatives and military actions hadn't been properly coordinated in support of one another. He spoke of Yitzhak Rabin and how he talked of renouncing violence and how violence undermined democracy. He mentioned Rabin's refusal to wear a bulletproof vest and told how a handwritten and bloodstained poem of peace had been found in his pocket after his assassination.

I asked about newly constructed Jewish settlements on the West Bank and what effect he believed these would have on any future settlement between the Palestinians and Israelis. He believed there should be a moratorium on any new settlements and that existing ones should be negotiated as any part of a future peace initiative and settlement.

His final words to me were, "I want peace for my five grandchildren. They should know peace in their lifetimes." The man said this as he stared off into the distance.

His words made me feel I had completed my quest for universal understanding. I had heard these same words in Syria, Lebanon, and now Israel.

The issue of establishing and expanding settlements in the occupied lands is a divisive one and, until the issue is resolved, I doubt there will ever be peace between Israel and its neighbors. Understanding the political structure and system in Israel makes it easier to understand why Israel has turned a blind eye to the expansion of settlements for so many years. Unlike the United States, which has only two major political parties, Israel, on the other hand, has many political parties. To form a government it's necessary to form a coalition between many of these minority parties. This requires that the ruling party agree to many of those personal agenda items that each minority party wishes to put forth as a condition of throwing its support behind a ruling party.

Some Jews in Israel believe that God had given these occupied lands to them, as a promised people. I believe that in order to avoid losing the support of minority parties, a blind eye has been turned to the practice of expanding Jewish settlements and other issues through the years.

Just as the United States has paid a price for turning a deaf ear to world opinion when it comes to its Middle East policies, I believe that Israel, too, has paid a price for its policies. A wedge has been driven between the United States and its European allies because of unilateral policies in the Middle East. Turkey has been traditionally a strong supporter of both Israel and the United States, but has recently become divided by the same issues facing the European partners. Just as the world has become a more dependent global economy, I believe there is ever-increasing importance on political globalization. Economic globalization and political globalization must reinforce one another if peace is ever to be sustained throughout third-world countries

A few days before we left Israel, a sailmaker came to *Tahlequah* to discuss providing me with new sails. He struck me as a sincere and honest man whom I could trust. I say trust, because I would take delivery of his sails in another country and would have to rely on his ability to make them right the first time. His prices were excellent, and he promised free delivery to Turkey, and because he was changing over to a premium (North Sails) sail loft, he was anxious to get the job. Although I wasn't looking for new sails at this time, I nevertheless needed to replace them.

How could I refuse such a deal? I thought to myself. I gave him a deposit, and we shook hands. Because he intended to send them to Turkey aboard a transiting yacht, he couldn't assure me where in Turkey exactly they would be delivered. I agreed to the conditions, and he promised me I would receive the sails in early September. Agreeing to our terms and conditions, I awaited my new sails.

While at the Herzliya Marina, I met a man and his wife from Holland who kept their sailboat there. In our discussions about the Eastern Mediterranean Rally, our visit to Israel came up.

"I lost my entire family in Holland during World War II and now have a home here in Israel. The people in Israel are warm and friendly, and I am happy to live here," the man said.

"The people are warm and friendly, but we weren't in Israel or, for that matter, Syria or Lebanon long enough to get a true sense of the countries."

"Do I sense you had a problem?" the man asked.

I was amazed at his ability to pick up on the fact that I was attempting to avoid any criticism, and he had immediately sensed something was wrong. Seeing an opportunity to let my guard down and just be open, I took a chance.

"As a matter of fact, I did have a problem. Some of us on the rally were uncomfortable with the unreasonable security measures. Kids running around with automatic weapons, out of uniform, everywhere. Hasidic Jews wearing sidearms. Fences creating camps keeping Palestinians in and out." I found myself on a roll and couldn't stop. "My female crew was harassed and mistreated by customs, and everybody seemed defensive in attempting to explain all these measures away. A part of me enjoyed Israel, and another part just wanted to get away." I could tell the man was patiently waiting for me to stop but was intent upon not interrupting me.

"I want you to return to Israel. I want you to stay with me and my wife. I promise you will see another side of Israel."

"I would enjoy that," I squeezed in between his words.

"Israel is many things to many people. First, you must understand that Israel is under siege by its hostile neighbors night and day. A day barely passes without a rocket attack and the threat of bombings. We have learned to live and adapt to constant threat from our neighbors. Israel exists because we have strong defenses and a strong military and strong support from the United States, our closest and only ally. Without tight security, there would be many more suicide bombings in Israel. As Israelis, we have learned to live with these measures out of necessity. These measures aren't directed toward you or other foreigners but, instead, out of necessity.

"Look, as for being defensive, maybe some of us are overly sensitive to world criticism and look to respond to it in the wrong ways. I don't approve of fences, but the government's argument is these borders are unprotected and used by terrorists to strike at Israelis and the very heart of our society. I hope that in the near future these fences can be removed. There is much more to Israel than what you experienced in a few short days. Return, and I guarantee we will see Israel together."

"You have my word on it," I said, sincerely planning to return in the future.

"Did you know that a few of Israel's greatest heroes were considered pacifists? You've heard of Moshe Dayan, the hero of the Six-Day War and legend of Israel for most of his life. Do you know what Dayan is known for? I'll tell you: he's known for dedicating the rest of his life to bringing peace between Israel and its neighbors. The same man that was responsible for taking Gaza and the West Bank was the same man who proposed sitting down with Israel's neighbors to negotiate a return of these lands for peace. People even began to refer to Dayan as *that Arab*. While others condemned him, he continued to work to bring about peace. There are other examples, but I want you to understand that there are those who aren't afraid to speak out in Israel and work toward a peaceful solution."

Although I needed time to consider his words, it was important for me to hear what he had to say. I was pleased to have an open and honest discussion with someone so willing to share his thoughts and with whom I could share mine. We continued talking for much of the afternoon, believing that someday I would accept his offer of hospitality and return to Israel.

CHAPTER 13

▼

THE LAST MILES

Sailing for three days and two nights, we arrived back in Girne, North Cyprus, en route to Turkey. It was here I became ill and was laid up for several days. Upon learning this, the marina operators took me to a local doctor for treatment. I was diagnosed with a viral infection. After I had received a prescription for antibiotics, they insisted upon paying my medical bill—I knew I was back in Turkish Northern Cyprus. It was here that Jackie left us to fly back to Turkey, in order to be there when her partner returned from consulting in Cambodia.

While in North Cyprus, Helen and I were introduced to the captain of an English-flagged mega-yacht berthed alongside *Tahlequah* at the marina. We were invited to the mega-yacht one evening for coffee. It was during a routine conversation that we learned the captain was a Kurd from Turkey. He described his difficulty in getting a job as a captain because of his Kurdish background. Although he had been encouraged to hide this fact, he felt he could not discredit his family and himself by lying and denying his Kurdish heritage.

After leaving North Cyprus, we sailed overnight to Kemma, Turkey. We had previously visited the Kemma marina months earlier for the purpose of deciding whether we wished to remain there with *Tahlequah* during the winter months. After visiting for ten days, we came to the conclusion that although there were large numbers of European live-aboards, it wasn't the lifestyle we desired. There were numerous activities and social occasions that we felt put pressure on live-aboards to participate in an endless string of activities. We believed that staying there would distract us from our desire to become absorbed into a local Turkish lifestyle and community. For this reason, we selected a marina along the Aegean and Ionian coast that consisted mostly of Turkish yachtsman.

Because there was no rush to return home, Helen and I decided to sail overnight along the Turkish coast, leave *Tahlequah* in a local marina, and see the wonderful area of Turkey called Cappadocia, which had a lunar-like landscape that had provided sanctuary to the early Christians who followed in the footsteps of St. Paul.

After several hours of driving en route to Cappadocia, we arrived, in the dark, at a small hotel. The hotel was built into one of the thousands of early Christian caves carved into the cliffs. The dining room was a deep cave with a hearth at the back. Tool marks were visible which had been left by the original inhabitants who had excavated the cave several hundred years ago. Handle-like protrusions had been carved into the cave walls to secure livestock. Here we enjoyed a wonderful traditional Turkish dinner by candlelight and fire in the hearth. The smell of smoke permeated the room.

At 3:00 AM, I was awakened by a strange noise coming through the cave walls. As sailors, we're accustomed to strange, unfamiliar sounds that alert us during the night. This sound was unusual and sounded like a metal tool clawing against rock. Without moving, I attempted to wake Helen, but to no avail.

The following morning at breakfast, others described how the same noise had awakened them during the night. One person was concerned the cave walls were shifting and on the verge of collapse. When we mentioned this to the proprietor, we received no satisfactory explanation. Metaphysical or geologic shifting—we'll never know the truth.

Following breakfast, we began our first day touring Cappadocia. The landscape was arid, consisting of strange, finger-shaped pillars scattered throughout valleys created by porous volcanic rock called tufa. Many pillars had doorway entrances to dwellings within. The erosion that had created this strange landscape began sixty million years ago. Recurrent volcanic activity, combined with local geological sediment, rocks, and lava eventually eroded from the weather to form this strange landscape. Early Christian Byzantine civilizations had created dwellings within these structures, which gave natural protection against invasion from other areas. Each community had pigeon coops carved into the hillside; pigeons passed messages from one area to another.

The next day, we visited the underground city of Kaymakli. Underground cities were used during periods of invasion. Villagers normally lived on the surface and relocated underground for up to several months during times of invasion. No underground city is believed to have been penetrated by invaders. Up to twenty thousand people (some estimate sixty thousand persons) at one time lived in these underground cities. We visited one of several underground cities and left with a true sense of underground existence. Although only 10 percent of the underground city was open to the public, we descended to the fifth level.

We were guided by an elderly English-speaking man who had been chosen by his village as their representative—a task he accepted with great pride. We saw family sleeping areas, chapels, areas reserved for livestock, burial areas, wineries, warehouses—all were methodically designed for convenience and protection.

Cleverly hidden air shafts descended to the lowest level of the city. Oil lamps and smoke fires were exhausted through an extensive array of camouflaged vents, making it impossible to see the city from afar. Although individual rooms were large, with high ceilings, the connecting passageways were very low, making it impossible for large numbers to storm the city from the surface. Large stone doors were positioned to block the entrances, preventing unwanted intruders and making the underground city impenetrable.

At the end of the tour, our elderly guide proceeded to walk to a nearby table to sit and order tea. As the others were busy continuing to explore the area, I asked the man if I could join him in having a cup of tea.

"Sure," he said.

"Where are you from?" the man asked.

"America."

"I went for tank training in America. Almost forty years ago now." The man spoke proudly. "You must be proud of your young men in Iraq. I know I would be proud if my son was there," he added.

"Americans are very divided on the Iraq war," I said, hoping I could avoid bringing my own personal feelings into the discussion.

"Yes. But what are your feelings?" the man persisted.

There was no point in trying to avoid his question any longer. "My wife and I are Quakers," I said.

"Who are they?" the man asked.

"It's a Christian religion and they're pacifists. They don't believe in wars or fighting as a solution to conflict."

"I see," the man said, seeming to accept my explanation at face value.

I was relieved when, at that moment, another tour bus arrived, and the man excused himself to greet another busload of tourists and show them the underground city.

Leaving the underground city, we drove past cave villages, some of which were inhabited by local families. As we passed one remote area, I asked our guide, Mustafa, to drop Helen and me off, allowing us to walk through the village alone.

After a long walk along a hillside, Helen and I came to one cave dwelling with a wooden ladder near the entrance. A young woman waved to us, and realizing she was beckoning to us, we proceeded to go to her home. When she invited us inside for a cup of Turkish tea, we discovered she spoke limited English. Her parents were out working in the fields and wouldn't return until late in the evening. The home had been carved from pumicelike stone many centuries before and had likely supported hundreds of families. It had no electricity, a small wood-burning stove for cooking, and kerosene lanterns for lights. A bathing basin was located in one corner of the small room. Scattered around the floor were many handwoven Turkish carpets. Goats were grazing outside, and their milk was used by the family.

Wanting to know more about the family living in the cave, I asked, "Do you live here year-round?"

Just then, I heard a baby's cry from a cradle in the corner. Rushing to pick up the baby, she gave it a bottle.

"Is the baby yours?" I asked.

"Oh no, it's my little brother. He's only three weeks old," she said, while holding the baby tightly against her bosom with one hand and holding the bottle with the other.

"Are there other children?" I asked.

"Oh yes, six, but they are still at school," she said.

"Have you always lived here?"

"My family has lived here for many generations," she said proudly.

"You don't have electricity; how do you stay in touch with the outside world?"

"Sometimes my father brings home a newspaper, but not too often," she responded.

"Do you have plans for the future?"

"Oh, yes. Someday I will marry and have my own family," she answered

"Yes, but do you have any other plans?" I attempted to ask without appearing to be looking down upon the merits of marriage and children. After a few moments, I could tell from her expression she was having difficulty coming up with something. Finishing our cup of tea, we thanked her for inviting us into her home.

On return to our cave hotel, we stopped along the roadside to take pictures at a scenic overlook called Fairy Chimney. A young family selling Turkish items greeted us. From them I purchased a headdress and invited the young family to pose with us for pictures. They had a young daughter who appeared to be as enthralled with our Western look as we were with her look. Each time I bent down to examine something on their table, she was intent upon reaching out to touch the broad brim of my bush hat. Helen purchased a handmade shawl from the young woman.

Each afternoon, I insisted upon eating at local restaurants where Turkish people ate. Often, we were approached by the proprietor, who asked where we were from. Frequently, this led to discussions about the area or the type of food locals ate. It was a wonderful experience, one that contributed to our understanding of local Turkish people and customs, and it was an opportunity for them to learn about us. I discovered that the longer I could manage to drag these conversations out, the greater chance I had of an open and sharing dialog between the restaurant proprietor and myself. On occasion, these interactions gave us an insight into the locals' daily lives and what their priorities, hopes, and dreams in life were.

On our final day in Cappadocia, while we were having lunch, the local restaurant proprietor joined us at the table. At one point in the conversation, he said, "In our newspaper we read about America violating the Geneva Convention in their treatment of captured soldiers. Is this true?" he asked.

I was taken by surprise and had to stop eating for a minute, just to swallow. "I guess you are referring to waterboarding?" I said, knowing well that it was a technique used to simulate near drowning.

"Yes, that's what I read about, waterboarding. Does America really do these things to prisoners?" he asked.

I was taken aback and surprised. I thought I was asking the questions, and he had nailed me, throwing me off balance. "I think waterboarding is torture, and a lot of people in congress do as well."

"So, why does America do such things?" he asked earnestly.

Realizing this was a two-way discussion, I felt I owed him the same honesty he'd provided me. "Our president has redefined the definition of torture to interrogate terrorist prisoners." Before I could be asked another question, I added, "I believe this will stop when we elect a new president, within a year," and I hoped he would be satisfied with my answer.

"But it's a violation of the Geneva Convention," he said. "How can America set an example for democracy when it tortures people?"

I knew now he wasn't going to let me off the hook. The others sat at the table, staring at me, with smiles on their faces.

"A lot of Americans are unhappy about our leadership in Washington because of these things. Trust me, Americans will vote for change in our next election."

"I hope so," the man said.

Appearing to be satisfied with my answer, he stood and began to clear some of the empty dishes from the table. Although the man wasn't smug or abrupt, I felt disturbed that I didn't feel I could defend my own country in light of something so terrible. Even worse, I was aware that recently published surveys showed that only 12 percent of the Turkish people, down from 72 percent only a few years ago, continued to support the United States. I was concerned that practices like waterboarding weren't doing anything to improve America's image abroad.

Returning to the marina, we resumed our ongoing trip home aboard *Tahlequah*. Our next stop was the area known as Kekova Roads with its underwater ancient city. Even to this day nobody has discovered who lived there. We dinghied across the bay to the ancient village of Kale Koy, an early pre-Christian community. Many of the original homes remained and people still lived in them. Narrow, winding streets littered with carpet shops and other shops rose along the hillside almost to the castle above.

Two young girls aged around nine and eleven, speaking limited English, followed us to the top, hoping to sell us handmade jewelry made by their parents. The young girls wore traditional Turkish dress, baggy colorful pants, and kerchiefs. It was a hot afternoon, and the girls accompanied us to the top carrying heavy straw baskets of items for sale. We implied we would purchase some trinkets when we returned. Not wanting to lose the opportunity of selling something, they continued with us to the top. The panoramic view from the castle overlooking the bays was indescribable. As we looked down, we saw *Tahlequah*, along with many Gullet yachts, anchored in the bay below.

When we returned to the village, Helen purchased handmade bead bracelets and a headscarf from one of the young girls. The other couple we were with informed the other girl they wouldn't purchase anything. The young girl begun to cry and ran to her mother, who was now standing nearby. Helen and I felt terrible and wondered why the couple we were with wouldn't buy something for 1 Turkish lira (75 cents), considering they had led the young girl to believe her efforts would be rewarded. Discussing this later, Helen and I wondered how many times foreigners come as guests to a country, took something away and left only bad will in its place.

Walking through a tented area referred to as a souk, Helen purchased more Turkish clothing. You remember the story of "Ahmed from America." Well, the wife of Ahmed from America must wear Turkish clothing, so Helen fulfilled her obligation to support the local economy and bought the colorful baggy pants many Turkish women wear in the countryside.

We enjoyed lunch in a small village restaurant overlooking the harbor. The restaurant owner warned us to leave immediately, as the wind was increasing, and waiting would be dangerous. Donning our foul-weather gear, we climbed into the dingy and began moving toward the entrance to the inner harbor. As we approached *Tahlequah*, the waves began washing over us, and we began planing at high speed to stay atop the waves, but progress was slow. Saltwater sprayed into my eyes, causing them to burn, making the trip more difficult. We negotiated behind small islands when possible to provide cover from the breaking seas and high winds. The outer bay, because of a two-mile fetch, encouraged waves to build during these conditions. Although we were drenched, once we were inside the harbor conditions quickly improved.

We had planned to remain in Kekova Roads for two days, but we were trapped and had to remain until the weather improved. Each day, we awoke to beautiful clear skies and sunny, calm conditions. However, each day at 10 AM the wind began howling. The sound of wind in the rigging competed with the noise of swells slapping the hull. In the morning, we went into town to grocery shop, buy fruit and vegetables at curbside stands, and enjoy a Turkish coffee before returning to *Tahlequah*. Here we met Hassan, the owner of a restaurant located along the waterfront.

His young daughter frequently played with other children on the dock, jumping in and out of the skiffs tied alongside. There was no need to warn these children of the dangers of playing on boats or docks. Like their parents before them, Turks learned from the sea and developed a love and respect for it from early childhood. Parents appeared comfortable with young children jumping into the water to recover a lost shoe or other item.

Hassan's wife, a beautiful young woman, prepared food in the kitchen and waited on tables. She didn't wear the traditional kerchief on her head. Her beautiful black hair flowed down past her shoulders and swished in the air each time she turned. On occasion, her young daughter returned to her mother for a comforting hand. Although I couldn't understand the words spoken between them, the loving relationship between mother and daughter was apparent.

Each morning Hassan, his wife, and daughter motored to our boat to deliver fresh-baked homemade bread as a gift to us. I observed that Helen and the woman appeared to take a liking to one another, as they frequently glanced at one another and smiled.

I learned later that Hassan's wife, Ada, had arranged to have breakfast with Helen in her restaurant. The next morning at 7:30, Hassan and his wife came to deliver fresh-baked bread to *Tahlequah*. She motioned for Helen to step into the boat, and then they sped off back to the restaurant for breakfast. When Helen returned, I asked her what it was all about. Helen said Hassan and Ada were discussing moving to America.

Apparently, Hassan had an uncle living in California, and he would sponsor their family to immigrate. Because his uncle had his own business, he would hire Hassan when he arrived. Ada wanted to talk to her about life in America.

"What did you tell her?" I asked.

"She's a woman; I told her the truth. I said it would take time for her to fit in, and if she made up her mind to be happy in America, she had a good chance of being successful. I said her children would adapt quickly and learn English from the other children. I suggested she sign up for English lessons as soon as she arrives, and everything else would fall into place. She asked me if it was okay to wear a headscarf in America, and I told her it was okay, but it would be easier for her to fit into American society if she did not wear one."

"Do you think that's true?" I asked Helen.

"As long as it's one of the colorful, pretty ones that she wears and not one of those black ones, with black clothes, nobody will care. She's a nice person, and once people get to know her, she'll be fine in America."

I couldn't help but wonder what it would be like to move to America as a Muslim in today's climate. Fine, I hoped, but I couldn't help but wonder about the problems she would have to face.

"But if she goes around wearing a headscarf all the time, do you really think she'll ever fit in?" I asked Helen.

"I hope so. Hopefully her husband's uncle will help them adapt and fit in. He's a businessman, and he did it, so she should be able to as well," Helen responded.

"Yes, but men don't wear headscarves. If she wears a headscarf, people might be suspicious of her. They will know she's a Muslim and probably think she's a terrorist as well."

"Now you're being silly. Who will think she's a terrorist just because she wears a headscarf?" Helen said.

"I hope you're right, but I think you're giving people too much credit. Everyone is suspicious of Muslims in the United States. Every night on the evening news, all they see is Muslim terrorists blowing themselves up. Then how about her children wanting to bring friends home? That will be another problem."

"What do you want me to tell her? Don't go to the United States?" Helen asked in a frustrated tone.

"Of course not! She will benefit from understanding the importance of fitting in and not separating herself from others."

"She's scared to death. She's never been out of Turkey, and she's very close to her family who live right here in the village … I kind of feel sorry for her."

"Maybe his uncle can help them adapt," I said in an effort to help make Helen feel better.

"I gave her my cell phone number and told her to call me if she has any questions. That seemed to make her feel better," Helen said.

"*Kewl*," I said. This was the signal word I always used, giving my thoughts away when I didn't quite agree.

I thought about the woman during the day and hoped all would go well for her and her husband. I never felt out of place as a Christian in Turkey, but I couldn't imagine what it would be like to be a Muslim living in America.

Maybe Helen's right, I thought. *Maybe I'm worrying about nothing.*

The weather improved enough for us to resume our trip home. In order to avoid overnight trips along the Turkish coast, we consistently stopped each day before sunset.

The following day we sailed to the Island of Kizilkuyruk. The anchorage was breathtaking and inhabited by only one other yacht, a Gullet. We anchored off a small sandy beach overlooked by steep rock cliffs, cascading from high above down into the water below. Goats foraged along the hillside, walking along small ledges jutting out from sheer rock cliffs above. One goat wore a bell, a signal to others that he was the leader and meant to be followed. Observing from the cockpit, we saw him return for an occasional young errant goat which had become separated from the others.

Swimming here in clear waters, through which the bottom was visible, surrounded by the beauty of nature—this is what sailing is about. Our anchorage was a peaceful place and one of the most beautiful anchorages we've experienced to date.

Helen and I planned to meet a good friend, a young Turkish captain of the *SV Infinity*, whom we had befriended a year earlier. We had kept in touch and planned to reunite in Gocek Marina for two days.

Entering the marina, we saw our friend Josuf was waiting for us on the dock. Josuf jumped aboard *Tahlequah* and kissed me on both cheeks, a greeting among Turkish men. He is a warm, friendly, and fun person, whom we had come to know when spending time together in Bodrum Marina the previous season. Josuf enjoyed cooking, and on occasion, he prepared a wonderful Turkish meal for us. Engaged to be married, he arranged for his fiancée to join us for lunch the following day. Over the next two days, we enjoyed many hours in the cockpit, talking about our past and future adventures.

Josuf will relocate his yacht to Istanbul, as the owner's wife is expecting her second child and doesn't wish to travel far until after the baby is born. We discussed meeting again at the end of June in Bodrum as he travels to Istanbul.

Josuf explained to us that he had no family, so the family of his fiancée was important to him. He worked with his future father-in-law to help replace the engine in his small fishing boat during his off-season. It was during this conversation that Josuf asked Helen and me to attend his wedding, and he said would like us to be his "parents" at the wedding.

At the time we weren't sure if we misunderstood his intention due to poor Turkish language skills on our part. We later learned that he did want Helen and me to be his parents at the wedding—we were both surprised and moved by his offer.

CHAPTER 14

▼

MAKING FRIENDS ABROAD

One man and his sister whom we came to befriend were of Turkish descent and also proud Americans. Ken was a retired U.S. Navy Seal. One Sunday afternoon, Ken picked us up at the yacht club and took us to his home in the countryside. It was a small hacienda-style villa with a high, white wall surrounding his yard. Entering, we were delighted to see many trees, flowers, natural streams, fountains, and a swimming pool. The house was a four-hundred-year-old cottage. He and his sister lived there half the year, returning to Miami, Florida, for the remainder of the year to escape the cold winter weather in Turkey.

Although originally Turkish, Ken was an American citizen and had been an officer in the U.S. Navy. He often wore a blue shirt and cap saying, *U.S. Navy Seals*. Inside his house, there were pictures of him with President Reagan, many senators and diplomats, and a certificate indicating he belonged to a Republican political organization. After retiring from the U.S. Navy Seals, he had become a councilor general to Turkey in the diplomatic corps.

There was no kitchen inside the house; all cooking was done in a special outside area reserved for this purpose. The kitchen countertops were constructed of stone and colorful tiles with several small gas-fired burners. They ate at a nearby table and chairs. This was a simple Turkish home, which he and his sister were proud of. Outside, on one corner of the house, was a sauna that Ken himself had constructed from cedar wood.

We observed that Ken and his sister, Baris, had successfully combined two cultures. In every way, they were Americans, but they had a proud Turkish past and heritage. This was evident in their lifestyle. The furnishings within the cottage were strictly Turkish. Ken described which area each piece of furniture had come from and how some areas of Turkey were known for these pieces.

Friendships are an important part of life, regardless of whether one is at home or on the road. Friends can be made anywhere, I've discovered over the years, and in the worst of times they can keep us moving forward. A few weeks after the rally, we were reunited with our special friend, Laurie, a British sailor who owned and captained the sailing yacht *Ruby Royal*.

Although a small yacht, it had been commissioned by the Duke of Edinburgh. A black-and-white picture of the duke hung in the cabin. Laurie was eighty, but showed no signs of slowing down. His two daughters came to crew for their father on different occasions during the rally. I suspected they volunteered in an effort to prevent him from single-handing. Although Laurie was an experienced and qualified sailor, I must admit, it's always a relief having extra crew. Both women were wonderful and were immediately befriended by Jackie and Helen.

Laurie's daughters, Sue and Sally, were outgoing, gregarious women, who loved to sail and party. Helen, Jackie, Sally, and I frequently went out for drinks and sometimes dinner together in the evening. We enjoyed every moment of our times together, which sometimes went on into the late evening and early morning hours. We were aware that Laurie had lost his wife two years earlier, and she frequently became the center of our discussions. Sally made the comment that since her mother had died, her father was like a rabbit caught in the headlights. Because of our own tragedies in life, we understood Sally's comments and felt all the closer to Laurie.

Although we had planned to leave for places where we could anchor safely, we received weather warnings predicting fifty-three-nautical-mile gusts. We had learned years ago to avoid bad weather, if possible, in favor of better conditions and smoother sailing.

One week later the weather broke, and Helen and I left for an all-day sail to one of our favorite small Turkish villages. Laurie's daughter planned to leave to return home to the UK and rejoin her own family now that the overnight sails were completed.

Helen invited Laurie to *Tahlequah* each evening for drinks and dinner. Laurie always brought a bottle of wine, which we appreciated. We enjoyed hearing about his childhood World War II experiences in London and the places he and his wife of many years had traveled together. Helen and I often talked about how we enjoyed evenings with Laurie and how we hoped we could spend many more hours together in the years to come. He was a unique person, a kind person, and one who enjoyed the company of others.

Over the years, I'd come to appreciate that a true friendship is rare. During my working days, I'd believed that some of my business friendships had become true personal friendships. It wasn't until after I'd retired at fifty-five and lost my son that I realized I'd confused business relationships with personal friendships.

For this reason, when I meet someone like Laurie, I appreciate our friendship all the more, because I understand now what friendship means. Helen and I have close friends we consider family—for example, Ivor and Bernice, who live in South Africa. They are our family—we don't need to be together each year or to talk each day. The meaning of our friendship is such that, when we are together, it's as though time has stopped for us. Each time we're together our friendship is uninterrupted and continues. I know there is nothing we would not do for them, and there is nothing they would not do for us. Because of our friendship, I fly a South African flag on *Tahlequah*'s port spreader.

Helen and I have collected various items from all over the world. From each country visited, we have brought back something we believed represented the country and these items are prominently displayed in our new home. From Israel, we brought back a mezuzah and a menorah, and they are clearly visible to anyone coming to our home. It would be easy for guests to make the assumption that we are Jewish. Although we have had many Turkish guests to our home, including friendly neighbors, we have never been asked about our religion, nor have we had reason to suspect any change in attitude toward us.

We befriended a Turkish neighbor, a single woman who had been an English instructor at a Turkish university. After learning that she spoke English, we depended upon her for translating, but as we came to know her better, we developed a friendship. Guliz was an intelligent, progressive, modern-thinking woman, interested in politics, and she never hesitated to share her opinions. Like Anna, our eastern Turkey guide, Guliz, our neighbor, also held strong and passionate convictions about Turkey's movement toward a more conservative environment.

One afternoon Guliz invited us to attend a neighbor's wedding. Knowing we had to first purchase a gift of gold for the bride, we went into town to a jewelry store. This is an old Turkish custom. Each guest pins something made of gold on the bride, known as the *bride's gold.* The gold belongs to the bride and can be used only by her for any purpose. Settling on a plain, gold bracelet, we went to the wedding.

The wedding was poolside at a large luxury hotel. After dinner, the band played lively Turkish music. A line of young Turkish men began to dance together. As the music became faster and faster, the men circled the room in a synchronized fashion and in perfect harmony. The dancing was similar to Greek dancing but with a Turkish flavor.

As the men stamped and moved rhythmically around and around, Guliz danced with her arms raised into the air, as if beckoning some unknown spirit to join her. The music and the sight of the dancers were intoxicating. It was hard to resist joining in on the evening's festivities. The essence of Turkish culture expressed itself at this moment without the need of words. Helen and I stood, happy that we could be a part of what was happening.

Now that the Eastern Mediterranean Rally was finished, Helen and I returned to our home in Bodrum, Turkey. As promised, and on time, I received a phone call from the sailmaker in Herzilya, Israel. My new "north sails" were completed and ready for delivery. He informed me that two Israeli women were coming to my marina to participate in the Women's International Race Cup. Informed that they were bringing my new sails, I offered to meet them at the airport and provide transportation. Seeing the sails, I was astounded that they had gotten them to the airport and through customs.

They had explained to customs that they were here to participate in the International Women's Cup and that the large bags contained sails. Customs allowed them to bring the sails into the country without additional duty. It's always amazed me what beautiful women can get away with. The sails were exceptional, high-quality, and the sailmaker had included, without additional cost, a zippered stack pack to protect the sails. When I learned that the sailmaker would be coming to Turkey in the future to investigate opening a sail loft, I invited him to stay with us.

A hotly contested topic involving Turkey in recent years is the Armenian accusation of genocide by France and, more recently, the United States. This subject again surfaced when the U.S. House of Representatives approved sending a nonbinding resolution to the House floor for approval, finding its ally, Turkey, guilty of genocide.

Helen and I had been invited to attend a special party to celebrate the end of Ramadan (a month long period of fasting). Knowing we were from America, people asked if we were Democrats or Republicans. Knowing that Democrats were favored in Turkey, we had no hesitation about pronouncing our allegiance to the Democratic Party. It was only later that evening while watching the evening news, that I saw mass demonstrations in Istanbul, protesting the actions of the Democratically controlled U.S. House of Representatives, approving a bill accusing Turkey of Armenian genocide.

To understand how important an issue this is to the people of Turkey, one has only to look to the past. Because the Turkish constitution prevents accusations that bring discredit to the government, even authors have been legally prosecuted for such things as accusing Turkey of Armenian genocide. In the past, any criticism of Turkishness has been prohibited, and legal prosecution can result from this behavior. This is one of the laws presently awaiting revision before Turkey can join the European Union.

Knowing I could depend upon a Turkish friend, Uri, to provide a knowledgeable understanding of how Turkish people felt on this matter, I met with him for a discussion.

I asked about his feelings on this issue, and he began talking. "Listen, no one denies many Armenians died; it is a fact. It wasn't genocide, because, by definition, genocide targets all people of one ethnic group with the intention of wiping them off the face of the earth. This never happened in Turkey. During World War I, the Armenians along our northern borders sided and fought with the Russians against Turkey. Armenians were marched to other areas, and many, many died. These things are sad and shouldn't happen, but it was a war. Armenians living in other areas of Turkey were never moved or relocated."

"Why is there so much anger against the United States because of this?" I asked.

"Because we always thought of the U.S. as our friend and our close ally. You know that Turkey is the only friend the U.S. has in this part of the world. We provide them with airbases and airspace to take men and supplies to Iraq and Afghanistan. We have paid dearly at times on our eastern border for being a close U.S. ally. In the past, Israel, Turkey, and the U.S. were close allies. Now the U.S. has turned against us, and we ask ourselves, *What do we get out of our relationship with the U.S.?*"

"Why do you think the U.S. did this?" I asked, hoping to learn something new.

"Because they want to make life difficult for your President Bush, and the congress is now controlled by Democrats. That's why!" he exclaimed.

"What do you think will happen now?" I asked.

"Turkey is threatening to take action and has already recalled their ambassador from the U.S. They could sever their ties with the U.S. and prevent them from using Turkey as a staging area for the war in Iraq, but we will see. I don't believe in the end they will do this," Uri stated, changing the topic to the PKK.

"What else might happen?"

"In the past, Turkey has not invaded northern Iraq to pursue the PKK terrorists, only because the U.S. has appealed to them not to complicate matters in Iraq. Because of the U.S. accusing Turkey of genocide and the anger it has created, I don't think Turkey will listen to the U.S. anymore. There are now 100,000 Turkish troops poised on the Turkey-Iraq border. If they obtain permission from the Turkish parliament, they will do what's best for Turkey and not only the U.S. anymore."

I knew that although the government was under tremendous pressure to respond to the PKK terrorist attacks, it showed much restraint by attempting to exhaust all diplomatic options before committing military resources. I admired their restraint and could only hope that there would be an ultimate diplomatic breakthrough, which would save many lives.

Turkish people are very patriotic. There were parades almost daily to exert influence on the government to act against the PKK. We saw trucks with loudspeakers in the streets stirring patriotism. Turkish flags decorated every home and storefront. The government passed a law to prevent the news media from displaying any more pictures of wounded or dead soldiers to help reduce passions and gain the time necessary to implement a diplomatic solution. The prime minister of Turkey hoped to travel to the United States to meet with the president to discuss solving the problems resulting from the PKK terrorist attacks.

After a brief hesitation, and getting back to the Armenian issue, my friend went on to ask, "Do you realize that it was the Ottoman Empire who did this at the end of the First World War? It wasn't even our present Democratic Republic."

"Uri, when do you feel was the last time Turkey had a good relationship with the United States?"

"The last time … I'd say it was with Clinton. Since then, Turkey and the U.S. have been distant. I read in the newspapers that we no longer share intelligence, and even top government and military officials no longer have links of communication with Washington."

"I've heard the European Union make similar complaints. The point I wish to make is that U.S. diplomacy will change during the next election. When that happens, not only Turkey, but the entire European Union, will reestablish relationships. I think that Iraq and the Middle East have occupied most of the U.S. attention at the expense of working with our traditional allies," I said. "I want to ask, other than national pride, how will this affect Turkey?" We were both now feeling comfortable, asking and answering questions.

His eyes swelled like saucers. "Look, Turkey is a poor country. This will raise all kinds of issues. There has been only one genocide in the last century—the extermination of the Jews. You would make this the second genocide. The U.S. will create a situation where legal suits could now be brought against Turkey, resulting in millions or trillions of dollars, while Turkey is a poor country. As a direct result of this, everyone fears Armenians will seek legal redress to redefine Turkish borders to create additional Armenian territories."

"I want to ask you a question," he said in a deep tone of voice, giving away the fact that he already knew the answer to his question. "If America is our friend, why would one friend do this to another?"

"I suspect this is all about internal American politics and has little to do with friendship or, for that matter, Turkey. I can't be sure, and I can't speak for the U.S., but I do believe it's a means of the Democrats slapping the Republicans and George Bush in the face. In the long term, I think it was a mistake to risk friendship over something that happened almost one hundred years ago and by another government."

"Don't you think the Trail of Tears, where many Indians died being marched across your country, was genocide?" he asked confidently.

"It was one of the great American tragedies, but by my understanding of the legal definition of genocide, I don't believe so," I said.

"Getting back to the Armenian issue, I listened the other evening to Jimmy Carter's comments on *CNN News* about whether he considered this genocide. He seemed appalled that the House would have approved such a declaration. I learned from him that every American president since Truman after WW II had to deal with the same Armenian issue coming before congress and that it has always been defeated. More importantly, he stated that the issue of genocide didn't belong in the U.S. congress, as they were a lawmaking body and not an ethical body to cast moral judgment on something that was done ninety-five years ago by a government that no longer existed. President Carter stressed that the U.S. had never passed a declaration against Nazi Germany because it was unnecessary—everyone knew what had happened. He also stressed that Turkey was a close NATO ally of the U.S., and they should be the last country to be treated in such a way."

"I agree, but if you understood the American political process, it would make sense," was all I could say in response to Uri.

Although this ended our conversation, Uri's answers were important to me, because I respected his opinions as a friend. I knew that whatever cross section of Turkey his opinions represented, they would continue to resonate within me.

There are many reasons to live in a foreign country. For Helen and me, it was more than the natural beauty, shoreline, or even plentiful antiquities, historical sites, and way of life found in Turkey. No, it was much more than their sum. We decided to make Turkey our home because of the extraordinary people.

Many Europeans have purchased homes along the coast of Turkey. In recent years, even small Turkish villages have attracted land developers, who have constructed condo-like structures to satisfy the demand of this expanding second-home market. For Europeans, this is an affordable investment and relatively inexpensive when compared to European homes of similar size. Expatriates are attracted by reasonably good year-round climate, beautiful shorelines and beaches, good food, and a very safe, politically stable life.

Few Americans live in Turkey when compared to their European counterparts. Because the U.S. dollar is weakened at this time, the cost of living is similar to the U.S., but not necessarily less expensive. While the cost of housing may be less than in the U.S., other costs, such as fuel, now valued at US$7.50 per gallon, offset these benefits.

Although Turkey is 99 percent Muslim, there are few indicators, other than an occasional attractive headscarf, that they are different from any European country. Of course, this is true along the coastal regions of Turkey, but it does not apply to all other regions of Turkey, especially those eastern regions.

At the beginning of Ramadan. I was awakened at 3:00 AM by someone beating upon a drum. Although this went on for only five minutes, I found it difficult to return to sleep. This continued each day without fail, and after a week, I decided I must have offended a neighbor, who was having his revenge upon me. In desperation, I went to Guliz, our Turkish neighbor, asking her, "Do you hear that drum every day at 3:00 AM?"

"Oh, yes. I put in ear plugs," she said.

"Is someone angry with me?" I asked.

"Angry with you? Oh, no!" she exclaimed. "It's tradition," she added.

"Tradition? What kind of tradition is banging on a drum outside my bedroom window at 3:00 every morning?" I asked.

"We've always done that. Because you can't eat after sunrise during Ramadan, the drum is intended to wake everyone up to prepare their meal early."

"You've got to be kidding," I reacted.

After receiving her explanation, I was no longer disturbed by the beating of the drum. I simply began to accept it as custom and tradition. A week later, my doorbell rang. Outside were three men, one with a drum, asking for a donation. I gladly made our donation to the three men to compensate them for waking me every morning at 3:00 AM. For a brief moment, I considered giving them extra if they would find another place rather than outside my bedroom window, but I thought better of it.

The final day of Ramadan is known in Turkey as the Sugar Festival and can be compared to Christmas Day for Christians. Sugar Festival is a major holiday and can last from three days to a week, depending upon the moon and how it falls over a weekend. Not understanding the tradition of Sugar Festival, we began the day by going to the post office to send off mail. When we arrived at the counter, we were invited to take a piece of candy from a large bowl. For the remainder of the day, everywhere we went we were presented with sweets.

Returning to our *sitesi* (gated community), we were greeted by a guard we had never seen before. Instead of opening the gate, he attempted to tell us something we didn't understand. Repeating again and again, "Please open the gate; we live here" brought no better results. Finally, he pointed toward the area near the office, where we saw a party going on. Once we acknowledged our understanding, he opened the gate for us to enter. Men, women, and children were all well dressed. After parking our car, we went to the party, where we met several new Turkish English-speaking residents. In typical Turkish fashion, many went out of their ways to communicate and be friendly to us. Unfortunately, we ate much more than we needed to. We enjoyed especially the baklava and other sweet-tasting foods.

Later that day, we received a phone call from our close friend, Josuf, the commercial sailboat captain of the private yacht *Infinity*. We were formally invited to his wedding in the coming week. When the day arrived, Helen and I traveled to Gocek by bus, where we were met by Josuf and taken to a comfortable local hotel. We were taken to meet the bride's family, where Helen was introduced as his mother.

Village weddings in Turkey are three days long, so we made arrangements to remain for two days and return home on the third day. The evening of the first day, we went to the bride's village. The street where she lived was closed off, and a band played Turkish music. The side streets were reserved for the men, who wished to separate themselves and have a drink of ouzo (Greek) or raki (Turkish) with other men. Helen and I joined the festivities with the bride and groom on the main street. There were at least two to three hundred people in attendance. Everyone danced to the lively Turkish music, and it was clear that all the people, including young children, were thoroughly enjoying themselves.

At one point, the bride sat with the groom in the center of the street, where a red veil was placed over their heads. One by one, people approached and pinned gold coins onto the bride's dress, offering their gifts of "bride's gold." Following this, henna was smeared on the hands of everyone as an offering of good luck from the bride to the guests attending her wedding. It's an ancient custom that continues to flourish to this day. Many times during the evening, Josuf came to us to be sure we were both enjoying ourselves. There was no question that this would be a special experience that we would all remember.

During the evening, I was asked to dance by several men, including Josuf. Like Greek dancing, it's a Turkish custom and one to be thoroughly enjoyed by all the wedding guests. On the second night, we gathered in a special enclosure in the center of the town near our hotel. Again, there were a few hundred guests. It was during this ceremony that the groom and bride were married by a Turkish government representative, as required by law.

After the wedding ceremony, the Turkish music began and continued all evening. After Josuf danced with his bride, he then announced he would dance with his mother, Helen, and I would dance with his wife. It was an experience that we will always remember and one we truly cherished.

Later in the evening, there was a professional dance troupe that did Turkish dancing to entertain us all. Afterward, the dancers went into the audience to get guests to join in. That night we left the wedding feeling we were truly Josuf's parents.

CHAPTER 15

▼

CONCLUSION

Each time I left a country, I departed with a simple, but growing, understanding of what the country's problems and difficulties were. As I moved from country to country, I began to realize that I became empathetic with each one I visited. One event more than any other helped me understand how the subtle clashing of cultures can result in stereotyping and misunderstanding. On the evening *EuroNews* report a journalist interviewed a German politician who blamed Turks living in Germany for not aspiring like other Germans to enter college and improve their lives. The politician accused them of placing more emphasis on family responsibility and honor than education. The journalist appeared bewildered by this answer and, after a brief silence, said, "Well, there is something to be said for family responsibility and honor." And with those words the journalist signed off.

Clearly, the intention of issuing travel warnings is to protect United States citizens abroad. Whether these warnings have been misused for political advantage, I will leave to the experts to decide. I can say that, in more than one country, I have been dismayed by these warnings and have had to wonder why I would be safer returning home.

Moreover, I have yet to see the United Kingdom or the States warn foreigners not to visit their countries immediately following "high alert" conditions or terrorists carrying out threats, as in the case of the London bombings or 9/11.

I recall one day, in Trinidad, seeing an American travel warning for all U.S. citizens posted by the United States Embassy on the marina information board.

There could be no question we were safer there than in some U.S. cities, given recent crime statistics released by the FBI. Tourists leaving the U.S. have little choice but to take seriously these warnings for their own safety and the safety of their families. People already in these countries, who are familiar with actual conditions, frequently integrate their best assessment with governmental recommendations when making decisions.

It occurs to me that, as I traveled around the world, people gave Helen and me the benefit of separating us from the politics of our home country when they took exception to our country's actions. Needless to mention, we always felt welcome everywhere we traveled.

When I first started writing, I wanted to contribute to the readers' understanding of the world. I didn't want to write a travel guide—but instead a validation of how the Western world forms preconceived ideas of third-world countries. If I have accomplished nothing else, I hope my effort has left others with the notion that most people in the world seek peace and reconciliation. Most people put their families' well-being before other issues. We have much more in common with people from countries that we are sometimes led to believe are villainous.

I'm aware that the news media feel they are charged to report national events and catastrophic disasters, believing there is little interest in the everyday life of normal people. After all, what sponsor would pay large sums of money to bring us the mundane, everyday thoughts of people like ourselves? Instead, we learn about faraway places from the views of the leaders of their country or ours.

Earlier, I talked of developing an empathy with other people around the world as a vehicle to better understanding their way of life and, perhaps more importantly, how to relate to them. Are Iranians, Syrians, and Lebanese any less human than we are? Do we not hear their individual voices—no matter how faintly— calling for peace throughout the world? Isn't the next step to respond to these calls before responding to the drums of war and conflict?

Someone once told me that a great orator begins first by becoming a great listener. We must listen to those whom we would call our enemies if we are to speak to their needs, so that, one day, they will become our allies and friends.

Traveling eliminates the filters placed between us and other peoples by society and governments. Traveling allows us to directly communicate with others and become ambassadors of goodwill throughout the world. Traveling allows us to contribute to change through empathy and understanding, and it may be a first step and vehicle toward world peace.

I'm convinced more than ever of the importance of offering those who are most vulnerable an alternative to violence as a solution to their problems. Just as terrorists have learned to reach out to recruit those searching for a means to change their lives, Western governments also have to learn to make available even greater and more desirable opportunities for change.

Fighting terrorism isn't only about killing and punishing those who have nothing to lose. We must move toward providing solutions for change that are all-inclusive and which will guarantee results without the use or threat of violence. Eliminate hopelessness and replace it with a vision of a better future, and terrorism will become a thing of the past.

Most of the world's population has little sympathy with the parochial mentality of politics and is concerned first with meeting the basic needs of their own families. As I travel around the world among third-world countries, I hear again and again the failure of governments to provide for and meet the needs of the common people. How often I hear from politicians that there are people who hate freedom and want to defeat our democratic way of life. To them I say, before one can be free, one must be fed. Change in governments and political ideology mean little to those who are poor and hungry.

Understanding the prevailing mentality of those we call enemies of our way of life is a prerequisite to ultimately finding a solution to a common problem. A hungry man cares little for democracy, socialism, or even communism. He cares only for the change necessary to relieve his hunger. The promise of change can give him hope for the future. We must not fail him, for if we do, he will become our enemy.

A major change in today's world is the Internet—a resource once available to only the top few percent of the world's population. What has changed in third-world countries is the availability of affordable Internet cafes and the comfort of a younger generation in using computers—these young people represent the future of their societies.

Internet cafes have sprung up throughout third-world countries, and governments are having an increasingly difficult time restricting usage and applying censorship, as new technologies expand the sharing of information. The Internet has become a tool of the masses, which allows people throughout the world to challenge their governments, share the truth about the violation of civil rights, and most importantly, influence and bring about change. A young blogger in Egypt posts videos of police brutality almost daily on his site and now enjoys almost one million hits a day. The government is now compelled to address this issue.

I see children in all countries not only playing computer games in Internet cafes but blogging and communicating with one another around the world. As a metaphor, I see the Internet as a form of traveling—in some cases, achieving the same benefits and results by visiting inaccessible places online. In the past, visiting such places was reserved only for those few who could afford to do so. Today, the Internet has allowed an entire new generation of explorers to travel throughout the world via cyberspace.

It is disheartening when major world powers prevent their citizens from traveling to countries, not because of concern for their safety, but for political gain. South Cyprus restricts travel of non-European Union members crossing from north to south. Many Middle Eastern countries deny entry to anyone who has visited Israel. The U.S. prohibits travel to Cuba and North Korea. In addition to outright travel restrictions, some countries discourage visiting other specific countries through the practice of such methods as strip searches and other means of intimidation upon reentry. These travel restrictions are but a few examples of a very long list of practices that violate the growing spirit of globalization in today's world. Unrestricted travel should be a fundamental right of all people. To restrict the right of passage of any person is a violation of that fundamental right. People who travel can change the world.

Because Helen and I own homes in Venezuela and Turkey, we are frequently asked by our American friends if we have felt at risk purchasing a home outside the U.S.

Some ask, "Aren't you afraid of anti-American backlash and for your safety?"

We're also often asked, "Have you considered your homes may be seized because you're American?"

We have to say that, yes, we have considered these things. We realize there are no guarantees that these things can't happen, no matter how low the risk. Then we add that we're not driven by the fear of what *might* or *might not* happen. We feel it's important to balance our lives realistically, enjoying the people and the places we visit and remain in. We can choose to surround ourselves with people we wish to have as part of our lives, and we don't have to live in fear of reprisals for expressing our thoughts and opinions.

As for our safety, I like to tell people the story of my experience in Japan, considered by many to be one of the safest countries in the world. In Tokyo, on a business trip, I passed through a Tokyo subway station only minutes before the fateful gas attack that resulted in the deaths of scores of people. Had I hesitated even briefly, I would have died. I can think of at least one more incident where I was at greatest risk in what was considered a safe place. This isn't to suggest that we should disregard our own safety. Instead, I am suggesting we follow our own leadings in life and not be driven by fear alone.

I found it difficult, when asking people questions, not to be influenced by my own biases and prejudices. While I want to remain neutral, putting this into practice is a real challenge. While most don't, I have seen some professional journalists fall victim to the same problem. My only excuse is I'm not a journalist—just a private individual interested in what others think.

It's impossible to travel throughout the world, as Helen and I have, and not be influenced by and become empathetic with those less fortunate than ourselves. It's impossible not to feel strongly when coming to understand and appreciate that there is no one solution to any one problem. Rather than draw my own conclusions for those who will read this book, I'll allow the readers to do that for themselves.

I've reminded myself that it was never my intention to uncover new worldwide problems or new opinions of the people who are a part of it. Instead, it was my intention to put a face and personality to the people who, although far away, are a part of our world.

Many of the world's greatest problems are the result of indifference and lack of knowledge. The world can be changed by those daring to be exposed to it.

Iyi yolculuklar. Yolunuz acik olsun
"Have a good trip. Hope you won't have problems on your way."

978-0-595-49930-4
0-595-49930-9